Spiritual but not Religious

SPIRITUAL BUT NOT RELIGIOUS

The Search for Meaning in a Material World

John Bartunek, LC, SThD

TAN Books
Charlotte, North Carolina

Cover design by Caroline K. Green

Cover artwork by lisima and agsandrew/Shutterstock

Library of Congress Control Number: 2019930595

ISBN: 978-1-5051-1355-6

Published in the United States by
TAN Books
PO Box 410487
Charlotte, NC 28241
www.TANBooks.com

Printed in the United States of America

Contents

Introduction

I grew up in an atheist family. We weren't militant atheists, but we never talked about God, prayed, or went to any kind of church. Well, I do remember going to a Christmas Eve service when I was four or five years old. And sometimes when I slept over at a friend's house on a Saturday, I would tag along with his family when they went to church the next morning. But in my formative years, the realms of religion were an unknown galaxy—I didn't know about them, and I didn't even know that I didn't know about them.

That changed when I was fourteen years old. I began attending a nondenominational church in the suburbs of Cleveland, Ohio, and I soon had a personal experience of God and became a believing Christian. So for me, religion—going to church, learning and acknowledging dogmatic teaching, engaging in specific rituals with other believers, and intentionally following particular behavioral norms—has always involved a personal choice and a spiritual experience.

During my college years, I met people who felt differently. They had grown up in religious households, but their religion had never felt spiritual. In fact, for many of them, the trappings of religion seemed to be an obstacle to real spiritual experience. They found spirituality outside of religion and in spite of religion. These friends sometimes described themselves as "spiritual but not religious."

Ever since, I have often puzzled over that phrase, and that reality. My own journey eventually led me to enter the Catholic Church, follow a call to the priesthood, and consecrate my life to God in a religious order. Each step of the way, religion and spirituality have always gone hand-in-hand. And yet, throughout my fifteen years of priestly ministry, I have continued to meet people for whom being spiritual seems more important and more real than being religious. And I have also continued meeting people who were outwardly religious but clearly unspiritual.

In my opinion, both "spiritual but not religious" and "religious but not spiritual" are incomplete. Neither gives the human heart the meaning we all long for. This book is an attempt to explain why. It is also an attempt to help religious people live more spiritually and to help spiritual people discover the incomparable riches of authentic religion.

1

What Do We Mean by *Spiritual*?

The word "museum" comes from a Greek term meaning "seat (or *place*) of the Muses." In ancient Greece, the Muses were nine goddesses, daughters of Zeus and Mnemosyne (goddess of memory). These Muses were the divine sources of inspiration for great artists. Using the word "museum" to refer to a place where we can study and contemplate great works of art illustrates the implicit connection between spirituality (inspiration) and religion (divine source of inspiration).

In fact, many of the greatest works in the world's best-known museums are explicitly religious in their subject matter and their origin, from Egyptian tomb decorations to baroque crucifixion scenes. Yet no one would claim that museum visitors must be religious in order to appreciate these great works of art. Somehow, their aesthetic eloquence is sufficient unto itself. The gallery of the Muses, then, is a safe place to explore the mysterious connections and distinctions between what is religious and what is spiritual.

Impractical Value

A museum also happens to be a quintessentially human thing. Unlike a burger joint, it has no obvious practical

1

purpose. In a burger joint, we can get food. We need food to stay healthy and alive. The practical purpose of a burger joint is undeniable. But what about a museum? The practical advantage gleaned from gazing at and thinking about a painting or a sculpture is less tangible. Some might even say there is no advantage. And yet, for more than a few centuries now, human beings have continued to pour immense amounts of time and money into the production, collection, and display of works of art.

The Detroit Institute of Arts, for example (I will be referring to many works in the DIA throughout these pages; I live nearby), ranks among the top six art museums in the United States. Its more than a hundred galleries host a collection whose net assets exceed $300 million. Its annual revenue in 2017 exceeded $55 million and covered its $40 million functional expenses.[1]

Yet no one eats its paintings. No one drinks its sculptures. No one lives under its roof, and no one weaves clothing out of the documents in its art reference library. What is so valuable about something so impractical?

In 2017, a recently rediscovered painting (just one painting) by Leonardo da Vinci sold at an auction for over $450 million, more than the entire asset value of the Detroit Institute of Arts. That broke the previous record held by an abstract landscape painting from William de Kooning called *Interchange,* which had sold for $300 million.[2] One single

---

[1]   "The Detroit Institute of Arts," Charity Navigator, accessed October 10, 2018, https://www.charitynavigator.org/index.cfm?bay= search.summary&orgid=3619.

[2]   Chris Harris, "Listed: The World's Most-Expensive Paintings Sold

painting, bought for as much as a record-setting Powerball jackpot. Why?

A Matter of Fact

A great work of art is worth more than the material used to make it because it captures and communicates—and sometimes symbolizes—something more than mere matter. A great work of art is like a sacrament: it mysteriously makes present through its physicality something that transcends mere physics. This is why human beings make art; this is why humans delight in beauty; this is why humans laugh at stand-up comedy routines and cry at sad movies; we, too, are more than mere matter.

I have never seen a squirrel contemplating a Rembrandt. I have never seen a dolphin attempt to capture a seascape in oils or watercolors. The arts—the creation of things like paintings, sculptures, and even films—is something uniquely human. Having food, clothing, and shelter is somehow not enough for us. Once we have supplied for our basic biological needs, we are still restless. This restlessness, this yearning for something beyond what is merely material, is the spark of spirituality. Every work of art is an expression both of the restlessness and of an insight or experience in which that restlessness was somehow recognized and relieved, even if only partially or temporarily. When we truly connect with a work of art, then, we are enriched by it in immaterial terms.

---

at Auction," *Living it*, accessed October 10, 2018, xhttp://www. livingit.euronews.com/2017/11/16/listed-the-world-s-most-expensive-paintings-sold-at-auction.

Surprised by Saint George

Have you ever been surprised in a museum? I have. In fact, the trajectory of my life was altered by a surprise encounter I had with a marble sculpture.

It was my junior year of college, and I was in adventure mode. I was in love with learning, with exploring and discovering. My history major and my university's myriad overseas campuses pointed me toward a year of study abroad. I started out in Florence, Italy, the birthplace of the Renaissance. My art history class was touring the Bargello National Museum, the medieval city hall turned priceless sculpture haven. Our guide led us into the Donatello room, and as the rest of my classmates followed the professor, my eye caught a marble figure in the corner that completely arrested my attention and irresistibly drew me toward it.

I stood before a life-sized statue of St. George whose presence was so compelling that it made me catch my breath. St. George had been a Roman legionary who became a Christian and rescued a Middle Eastern village from the tyranny of evil, usually represented in art and legend by a dragon. Donatello, however, chose to omit the dragon from his marble sculpture. Instead, he depicts George as a young soldier, wearing his armor and military cape, and balancing his shield on the ground in front of him. With his weight equally distributed on both feet, contrary to the more popular Renaissance trend toward the elegant, dance-like contrapposto position, the saint gives an impression of stability, firmness, and determination.

His head is turned slightly to the left as he looks into the distance. Whatever he sees, whether the dragon or something else, he is ready for it. His furrowed brow shows a recognition that the challenge ahead of him is serious. His slightly parted lips show an eager confidence instead of fear.

But that day, when this six-hundred-year-old sculpture seemed to tug at my soul, I perceived something even deeper than courage and strength. I saw in his face and his bearing something that I didn't find in myself, something that I longed for even without realizing it. *Purpose*. Joyful, vibrant, life-giving *purpose*.

Before going to college, my life's purpose had been clear: get into the best college I could get into. That goal shaped my decisions and behavior all through my high school years so that arriving to university was for me kind of like arriving to heaven. I threw myself into the joys of learning, free from pressure and worry. But by my junior year, heaven was halfway over. I had to make some decisions soon about what would come next. What criteria would I use for those decisions? I didn't know. I wasn't sure. I had no underlying purpose. I felt a strong aversion for any path that offered social acceptability and worldly success without also offering lasting meaning. I was thirsty for a meaningful way forward in life.

In the figure of St. George, I found a stunning depiction of someone who knew his purpose so clearly that every fiber of his being was fully engaged in carrying it out. That's how Donatello had understood the soul of this saint and martyr. I caught a glimpse of that, and it gave me hope: Someone had found purpose, experienced it, captured it, and communicated it in this sculpture. Purpose is real. Maybe I can find it too.

Purpose is not merely material. Meaning goes beyond matter. The thirst for meaning and fulfillment is a thirst for transcendent values, for goods that will last, unlike all the passing goods of the material world. We can get a taste of these values through encountering great works of art. These works are known as mighty achievements of the human *spirit* precisely because they are windows into the spiritual realm, the mysterious realm of those transcendent, supra-material values so much more satisfying than even the finest seven-course meal or the soundest night of sleep. In its most basic and general sense, that's what we mean by "spiritual."

2

What Do We Mean by *Religious?*

The word "temple" comes from the Indo-European root word for "clearing" or "space." The earliest temples were simply clearings in the forest where people would worship their gods. It was important to have a special place reserved for those activities because they were sacred, somehow separate from and more precious than normal, everyday, profane activities.[3]

Temples vs. Museums

The beautiful marble columns on an ancient Greek or Roman temple remind us of this original meaning. They reflect the columns made from tree trunks used in even more ancient constructions, which in turn echo the original forest context. Their capitals are like the spreading branches at the top

---

[3] For the historical data and interpretation used in this chapter and chapters 4 and 5, I am greatly indebted to the many works of Christopher Dawson, especially his two series of Gifford Lectures on Natural Theology published under the titles *Religion and Culture* (Catholic University Press, 2013) and *Religion and the Rise of Western Culture* (Image Books, 1991), as well his 1929 work *Progress and Religion: An Historical Inquiry* (Catholic University Press, 2001).

of a tall tree, reminiscent of the majestic oaks or sycamores that might have flanked a primitive temple clearing.

Reserving a sacred space for interaction with deities, or a deity, implies a recognition that those deities were somehow relatable, personal. But it also implies that they were distant, or at least resided in a different realm or dimension, a transcendent dimension.

Here we find both an element in common between spirituality and religion and also an element of difference. Each points toward transcendence, toward something greater than what we normally perceive and experience in the material world. Yet unlike spirituality in general, religion always populates that transcendent realm with personal beings. True, some religions view the transcendent in terms of impersonal forces, but even in that case, the forces can somehow be influenced; a relationship can be established that allows interaction between them and the people living in the material world who are somehow dependent upon them.

This helps explain why what happens in a temple is so different from what happens in a museum.

In a museum, we contemplate works of art. We read them and, in a sense, listen to them; we try to discover their message and allow them to touch our souls. We enjoy them—their beauty, their meaning, their inspiration. But we don't pray to them. We don't attempt to enter into a relationship with them—at least, that's not what museums are for.

Religion, on the other hand, is all about relationship. One theory about the origin of the word "religion" points out that it may come from a combination of "re" (a Latin prefix meaning "again") and "ligare" (a Latin word meaning "connect", as in ligaments). Religion is about establishing a mutual interaction with the beings who dwell in the realm of transcendence but who at the same time influence the material world, where people like us live their lives.

Religion From Beyond and Religion From Within

Because transcendent values resonate so much more deeply in the human heart than immanent values, the beings who live in the transcendent realm are thought to be that much more powerful than us. The things that change—the seasons, plants and animals, the very earth itself—are seen to originate from and depend on things that don't change, transcendent things.

It is no coincidence that humanity's earliest ventures in writing and science were linked to religion. It was the religious instinct, this vague but undeniable awareness of the transcendent, that moved our ancestors to study and record the patterns of change so evident in the material world. Finding ways to record the motions of the heavenly bodies gave rise to calendars, and calendars allowed for a more accurate prediction of seasonal and climatic phenomena, which in turn opened the door to enhanced agricultural techniques. The first literate groups in human history were the priests, who were also the first scientists. Somehow, the human mind's search for greater understanding of self and the universe was, originally, connected to the human heart's experience of awe and wonder in the face of nature's beauty and power.

Religion has always sought to know what the transcendent realm, and the beings who live there, are like. The answers to those questions gave rise to religious dogma, either mythical or doctrinal or both. Religion has always sought to establish ways of properly entering into relationship with the transcendent realm and the beings who dwell there. The rituals of worship and prayer, so varied throughout human history, have their origin here. They provide an avenue for communicating and interacting with the gods, the transcendent beings so evidently present behind the veil of the material world.

For many centuries, dogma and ritual were deemed sufficient. Then in the sixth century before Christ, a worldwide revolution in religion took place, weaving moral behavior into the religious outlook.

Confucius in China, Buddha in India, Zoroaster in the Middle East, and Socrates in Greece each independently and in his own way constructed a bridge between morality and religion. For them, ritualistic theogamy (the bringing together of this world and the transcendent realm) wasn't enough. It was too superficial. Evidence of transcendence could certainly be found in the material world, but for these religious revolutionaries, it could also be found within the human heart. We could touch transcendence by reaching out beyond the stars, but we could also touch transcendence by reaching deep within ourselves.

There we discover a mysterious spiritual depth, a limitless space of encounter and yearning where an inner voice guides and calls. Learning to hear and heed this voice became an alternative avenue for entering into relationship with what was lasting and fulfilling. And so moral behavior became a more explicit element in religion.

Religion thus took on its trappings: dogmas, rituals, and behaviors deemed worthy and fruitful for living in harmony with and tapping into the realm of transcendence.

Superstition, Spirituality, and the Search

When those trappings are present, but a living relationship with the deity is absent, we find superstition of one form or another. The superstitious believe that transcendent powers are influencing their lives, but managing those powers is more of a technique than a relationship.

Superstition can be connected with magic, tapping into unseen powers through esoteric methods. But it can also take the form of religious dutifulness. The dutiful are those who follow all the religious rules but have no real relationship with the deity they worship. It is religious compliance and achievement often, though not always, based on fear, but it lacks true religious companionship. The deity watches and judges, perhaps, but doesn't accompany. Dutiful believers check all the dogmatic, ritualistic, and behavioral boxes, but they don't share a life with the one they worship.

Superstition is at the root of those who end up religious but not spiritual. Somehow they have lost, or maybe they never had, the transformative spiritual experience of deep personal contact with real transcendence. The truly spiritual person will revolt at this kind of aberration. And it is an aberration. Religion without spirituality—rituals, dogma, and moral boundaries without an experience of transcendent beauty, truth, and goodness—is a lifeless shell of real religion.

And yet, spirituality without religion is also an aberration. This is less obvious, but equally true. In the wake of experiencing transcendent values, the human heart naturally yearns for more. We yearn to know the source of those values. We yearn to find a way to live more fully and more constantly in touch with those values. Any experience of transcendence sparks a desire to bring one's whole life—beliefs, practices, and choices (dogma, ritual, and morality)—into harmony and vibrant communion with that deeper reality.

Fulfilling that desire will require a search because the transcendent realm is mysterious, not easily fathomed. And since every search involves effort, not everyone who has a spiritual experience will follow through on it. Some will even stifle the desire in order to excuse themselves from the search.

Here we find once again the natural connection between spirituality and religion. Experiencing transcendent values opens our horizons to another realm promising greater fulfillment than the merely material. But an initial experience of that realm naturally leads to a search for greater communion with what it has to offer. *When the search produces results, spirituality blossoms into religion.* Yet if those results ever lose their relationship with the original experience and the subsequent search, the blossom fades or petrifies.

Healthy religion, then, is the natural outgrowth of authentic spirituality. They are linked by the search for transcendence that has always characterized the human spirit.

3

Two Paintings, Two Loves

In a small gallery of the Detroit Institute of Arts, two paintings hang side by side as if purposely arranged to show the intersection of spirituality and religion.

Talking Oak, a small nineteenth-century painting by William Maw Egley, depicts a beautiful young woman leaning against the trunk of a tree and gazing into the distance. Her face radiates joyful longing, glad desire, the fullness that comes from being in love—one of the most universal and irresistible experiences of transcendence.

Egley's painting translates into visual form a few lines from Tennyson's poem of the same name:

> Then flush'd her cheek with rosy light,
> She glanced across the plain;
> But not a creature was in sight:
> She kiss'd me once again.

The Oak Tree Talks

In the poem, an ancient oak tree speaks those lines. The protagonist of the ballad, a young man named Walter, often makes his way from town into the field where the majestic tree grows. There, addressing the tree, he would unburden his heart and speak of his love for Olivia, whose name he had carved into the bark of the tree. During one of these rapturous monologues, Walter suddenly hears the tree respond to his musings and questions. It describes all the people who had taken shelter under its shade and claims that none compares to Olivia:

> I swear (and else may insects prick
> Each leaf into a gall)
> This girl, for whom your heart is sick,
> Is three times worth them all.

On many levels, this painting exemplifies the spiritual dimension of the human experience. The theme of true love, present in art and literature since the dawn of history, is itself a window into transcendence. Anyone who has been in love understands how different the experience is than simple lust. To fall in love is to perceive another person's unique goodness and beauty so intensely that it changes everything. When we fall in love, we feel more alive, more powerful, more hopeful, and more purposeful. Through our encounter with the beloved, all that had been humdrum and material acquires a deeper meaning. Life becomes more worth living.

Talking Oak, both Tennyson's poem and Egley's painting, evokes this experience. Yet, it also unveils other levels of human experience also touching on the spiritual, the transcendent.

Here is how Tennyson describes Walter's frequent trips to speak with his confidante—the oak tree—outside town:

To yonder oak within the field
I spoke without restraint.
And with a larger faith appeal'd
Than Papist unto Saint.

For oft I talk'd with him apart
And told him of my choice.
Until he plagiarized a heart,
And answered with a voice.

Being away from the constraints of everyday working life
in normal society, Walter is able to freely express what is
happening not on the surface of his life and of his mind
but in the unseen depths: "To yonder oak within the field,
I spoke without restraint." Haven't we all experienced this?
At times, our hearts are so full and charged that we simply
must find a safe place to express ourselves. Tennyson uses
a religious comparison to describe the intensity of Walter's
experience: "And with a larger faith appeal'd than Papist
unto Saint." Just as devout Catholics pour out their souls in
prayer, convinced that God and his saints exist in an unseen
realm and will offer spiritual relief, so this young man pours
out to the venerable oak tree the abundance of feeling in
his smitten soul. Some human experiences *transcend* what
is mundane. They appeal to something beyond, something
more than measurable, material categories.

Choosing a gnarled oak tree as his confidante is signifi-
cant. In pagan religions, trees were often considered to be
the dwelling place of divinities. This sentiment overflows
from animism, which saw every natural reality as being animated by a divine being. In Greek mythology, for example,

dryads were nymphs who inhabited certain forests or trees, and oak trees were especially apt for this divine inhabitation.

A Special Place

Early Christian missionaries encountered pagan cultures where this kind of nature worship prevailed. St. Boniface's experience is perhaps the most famous. Around the year AD 722, he was continuing his missionary work among the pagan cultures of Germany. On the summit of Mount Gudenberg, according to the tradition, stood Donar's Oak, an ancient and sacred tree religiously venerated by all the surrounding peoples. In a public ceremony announced well beforehand, the Catholic bishop offered to prove that the pagan beliefs were mere superstitions by chopping down the tree. The large crowd expected some kind of divine punishment to fall upon the presumptuous Christian, but instead, after only a few swings of the ax, the tree collapsed and broke into four parts. The wood was later used to build a Christian chapel, a kind of evangelizing rendezvous for the area.

Why would pagan religions assign divine attributes to something as mundane as a tree? For the same reason that the love-stricken Walter "spoke without restraint" to "yonder oak within the field." The majestic tree gave off an air of permanence and stability amidst the relentless flow of time. When the tree begins to speak in the poem, it reveals a knowledge of many things linked to its age and awe-inspiring presence. Walter was drawn to it as to a place resonant with transcendent significance and reverence, a place worthy of the transcendent feelings he is experiencing.

We have all felt something similar at some point. We have found a special place, a place where it was safe, and somehow appropriate, to open our hearts, even if only a tree, or a mountain, or a garden, or a shore was there to hear us. This is the sense Egley conveys in his visual depiction of Olivia under the same oak tree.

The tree supports her, comforts her, as she leans on it. She is free under its protection, free to feel what she is feeling "without constraint," as Walter expressed it in the poem. She finds in this place an apt place for her heart to overflow. This aptness comes across visually through Egley's choice of colors. Olivia's golden hair is echoed in the soft yellow of the sun-drenched grass and tree trunk. The various shades of green in the leaves and the distant tree tops gently mirror the rich green satin of her blouse. The blue of her shawl and the white of her skirts reverberate through the white clouds and blue sky visible in the background through the oak's branches. Nature itself is in harmony with her own inner experience. This is what happens when the spiritual dimension of our humanity is somehow enlivened; we feel in tune with the universe, as if the hidden forces sustaining the world around us are suddenly on our side, gently but surely guiding the reins of our lives. This portrait of a young woman in love is a portrait of transcendence, of the intersection of the spiritual and the material in a pure and youthful heart.

A Devout Child

Right next to *Talking Oak* is a similarly sized painting called *The Devout Childhood of St. Elizabeth of Hungary* by Charles

Collins. Elizabeth of Hungary, a thirteenth-century noble-woman widowed after only six years of marriage, showed deep religious sensibility from an early age. This overflowed in a remarkable dedication to prayer and to serving the poor and the sick throughout her life, which ended prematurely when she was only twenty-four years old.

Collins's painting depicts a scene from Elizabeth's child-hood. He shows her dressed in royal blue, with the chain of office (she was the king of Hungary's daughter) around her neck supporting a golden cross. She has arrived at the chapel early in the morning, before the priests have even been able to open the door. Dropping to her knees, and letting her prayer book fall from her grasp, she leans longingly against the solid wooden door of the stone chapel. Only a small bit of countryside is visible in the background. Besides a little rosebush in full bloom next to the doorway, the entire paint-ing is filled with the girl's figure pressed against the imposing chapel structure. The focal point draws the viewer's attention to her face and her hand, the soft skin of her cheek and her palm are pressed firmly against the solid wood of the door, which has no handle and no window—it can only be opened from within. Besides the deep yearning to be inside, her face also expresses sadness, a fascinating characteristic to see on such a young girl's face.

This painting, like *Talking Oak* beside it, shows a young woman in love. But Elizabeth's love is different than Olivia's. Olivia is full of hope and joy at the prospect of soon being united with Walter. Elizabeth's yearning is somehow less optimistic. She is experiencing something much deeper than infatuation and the bud of romantic friendship encountered as a surprise and a gift. She is feeling an existential need for something she has absolutely no way of supplying herself. Thus, the yearning is poignantly combined with melancholy. She feels her need. She knows that only God, only the divine presence can fulfill it. And although she can press with her whole being upon the doorway to that presence, she must wait for the door to be opened, for the divine presence to let her in.

"A Trumpet Sounds / from the Hid Battlements of Eternity"

The human heart's religious longing is never fully satisfied in this temporal realm. The taste of transcendence that spiritual experiences give us here produces a curiously contradictory feeling: it satisfies us in ways that nothing merely material—neither pleasure, nor wealth, nor worldly achievements—can, and yet at the same time, it stimulates our thirst for complete union with the source of that transcendent experience. The goods of this world lose their allure in the wake of experiencing God, and yet while we still dwell in this world, our experience of God is never enough.

Mystical writings overflow with passionate attempts to express this paradox. St. Teresa of Ávila put it strikingly in a poem from the sixteenth century:

> Ah, how bitter a life
> When the Lord is not enjoyed!
> While love is sweet,
> Long awaiting is not.
> O God, take away this burden

> Heavier than steel,
> I die because I do not die.

We can imagine the small figure of Elizabeth at the door of the chapel feeling that bittersweet mix of satisfying love, of unspeakable joy—knowing how close she is to the renewal of her communion with God that will come from the Mass soon to be celebrated in the sacred space behind the door—that brings about its own burden ("heavier than steel") because it promises a consummation never fully obtainable on this side of eternity. Truly tasting the transcendence of God's love, but tasting it from a distance, having to continue this journey through time and space before being definitively united to that infinite goodness—this is a kind of death while still enjoying life: "I die because I do not die."

We can relate to this too. The most intense and satisfying experiences we have here on earth do not last. They seem to carry a message from a realm where they do last, a transcendent realm. But here in this world we only get glimpses, whiffs, hints. Francis Thompson captures this combination of sweetness and frustration when he writes:

> I dimly guess what Time in mists confounds;
> Yet ever and anon a trumpet sounds
> From the hid battlements of Eternity;
> Those shaken mists a space unsettle, then
> Round the half-glimpsèd turrets slowly wash
>   again.

Olivia was experiencing the fullness of life and love as it blossoms here in this world of time and space, and Egley's painting captures and celebrates that. Elizabeth, on the other hand, is hearing the "trumpet sounding" from the "hid battlements of Eternity": she is experiencing an existential thirst that she cannot deny, but a thirst that can only be partially slaked here in the merely human realm.

When we gaze at these paintings and let them speak to us, we encounter the intersection of spiritual and religious. The spiritual dimension separates humanity from the rest of the material world. Something in our hearts and minds seek and find a meaning deeper and broader than can be explained merely by chemistry and biology. This is the origin of poems and paintings like *Talking Oak.* The religious dimension takes up what is spiritual and questions it, explores it, probes it to uncover its origin and destination. The spiritual dimension sparks love that transcends mere affection and animal loyalty (a spouse brings a deeper connection than a pet); the religious dimension intuits that such a love must be rooted, somehow, in an even higher Love.

4

Aren't All Religions the Same?

If spirituality and religion are so naturally linked, why do so many people keep them separate? We have already briefly alluded to those who are de facto religious but not spiritual, those who find comfort and clarity in the trappings of religion—dogma, ritual, morality—but who live without the vibrancy of authentic spiritual experience. In my own interaction with people in this situation, I have found the disconnect usually extrinsic rather than intrinsic. People who overemphasize the trappings of religion have usually at some point had a profound spiritual experience, but they have forgotten about it. This spiritual amnesia can have many causes, some psychological and some moral.

Learning From the Pharisees

In the Christian tradition, the quintessential exemplars of this phenomenon are the Pharisees. This group of religious leaders in ancient Israel make numerous appearances in the Gospels of the Christian New Testament. Jesus converses and interacts with them frequently, always trying to jostle them out of their hypocrisy by reminding them of the real soul of religious experience. But their arrogance, subtly nourished over years of striving for religious perfection understood merely as obedience to external norms, makes them largely impenetrable to Christ's appeals. They had traveled a path of sincere religious devotion that gradually degenerated into cold and judgmental self-righteousness.

This often happens to sincerely religious people. The human heart is easily corruptible, and this is one of its corruptions. Unfortunately, pharisaical distortions of authentic religious experience can be offensive and alienating. Encountering pharisaical folks is often a major religious turnoff, and encountering religious hypocrisy can turn people away from religion altogether. Thus, those who have unwittingly become *religious but not spiritual* can also unwittingly inspire others to opt for becoming *spiritual but not religious.* Every action produces its opposite and equal reaction, as the physicists like to remind us.

But we can detect an interesting difference between those two groups. The Pharisees would never have actually *claimed* to be *religious but not spiritual,* since their religious practice originated with a sincere spiritual conviction. But many people do in fact claim to be *spiritual but not religious* and even wear it at times like a badge of honor. They welcome and value transcendent experiences, but they refuse, at least explicitly, to subscribe to religious dogmas, rituals, or moral codes that profess to explain and cultivate those experiences more fully. One of the most common reasons they give for keeping religion at a distance has to do with the contradictory claims between different religions.

Spiritual experiences, they reason, are common to people from many different cultures and religions. But the trappings of the different religions—dogmas, rituals, moral codes—contradict each other. Those contradictions create conflict that in turn obscures those spiritual experiences found at the heart of all religion. And so they wonder: *Can't we just stay with the spiritual experience and forget about the religious trappings that are always causing problems? Isn't the spiritual experience the same for all of us, and can't we just find common ground there and so avoid conflict?*

Beneath this line of reasoning is an assumption that in their substance, all religions are actually the same; the differences are only accidental. Those who have discovered the spiritual ground underlying apparent religious differences, then, prefer to stay there. Being spiritual but not religious is, for them, an escape from the maze of religious confusion that so often breeds pharisaical hypocrisy and stifles authentic spirituality.

We need to explore this line of reasoning a bit more deeply. If it is true, then being spiritual but not religious is really the only option for an honest person. But if it is false, then being satisfied with staying spiritual but not religious is *not* an option for an honest person.

The Elephant in the Room

A well-known old parable compares the many religions of human history with an elephant. The story goes that just as blind men touching different parts of an elephant may think they are touching entirely different animals (the leg isn't the same as the trunk or the ear), so too human beings invent different religions whose differences are only apparent. In truth, this theory proposes, all religions are basically the same, just as an elephant is really just one animal with many parts. If this were indeed the case, then reconciling the different religions would simply be a matter of greater mutual understanding, of removing the blindness of the individual religions so they can see the bigger picture.

This parable hopes to resolve the problem of religious differences, which really is a problem. Throughout history, religious beliefs have been invoked to justify such damaging creeds and behaviors as racism, sexism, classism, terrorism, war, and even genocide. In the name of religion, human dignity has at times been obscured and human rights violated or ignored. Religion has also inspired greatness—especially in the realms of art, science, drama, literature, and social cohesion—but that greatness can't undo that damage. This is why the problem of religious differences really is a problem.

Some would say that religion itself *is* the problem, that getting rid of religion altogether would remove the very source of humanity's strife and misery. In this case, reconciling religious differences would be unnecessary. Without an elephant, we wouldn't have any need for mutual explanations and understandings about different perspectives on the elephant.

Erasing Religion

In fact, recent history has witnessed social experiments attempting to erase religion from society. The leaders of the French Revolution clamped down on traditional French religion and attempted to replace it with devotion to human reason. They even enthroned a woman symbolizing reason in the Cathedral of Paris while persecuting religious adherents who refused to abandon their traditional beliefs. Similar governmental measures happened in Mexico and Spain in the early twentieth century. Chinese and Soviet communism engaged in comparable social experiments, enshrining atheism as an official state worldview.

These experiments were enabled in modern times partially because of advances in science and technology. Those advances seemed to provide real, measurable answers to many questions previously tackled by mythology and other superstition-saturated religious dogmas. The ancient Greek myth explained the earth's stability, for example, through appealing to a superhuman figure named Atlas, a Titan who joined the failed rebellion against the Olympians and was subsequently punished by having to hold up the cosmos on his shoulders for all time. With the scientific revolution, any literal veracity of such myths simply evaporated under the warm light of discoveries like gravity, elliptical orbits, and the earth's rotation. The undeniable explanatory power of modern science, so many thought, would gradually evaporate all superstitions in the same way. Religion, nothing more than a crutch for the unenlightened, would soon be cast aside altogether. Socio-political movements like the French Revolution and Soviet communism were viewed as accelerants, midwives that could help the birth of a new humanity, free of religion and therefore free of strife and injustice.

It didn't happen that way, however. Science and technology have continued to advance, but the answers they provide haven't quelled mankind's spiritual search. This is because those answers don't actually extend to the spiritual dimension. We can research what parts of the brain are stimulated by prayer and meditation, for example, but we can't seem to find a remedy to relieve our thirst for meaning, purpose, and other transcendent values. People still search for those things. People still need those things. And those things have an immaterial dimension, a spiritual dimension that can't fit inside a test tube or under a microscope. You can't just take a meaning pill to satisfy your existential need for purpose.

To be fair, many adherents to the science-will-evaporate-religion worldview claim that we are still moving in that direction; we just haven't arrived there yet. A little more time, a little more research, and we will indeed achieve the final breakthrough, eliminating once and for all religion and its impediments to Progress.

One could call this point of view truly faith-filled, almost like a new kind of religion that has put its faith in science, but still is animated by faith. The problem with such a religion is its self-contradiction. The scientific method by definition can only explain material things. Religion, in its essence, reaches after explanations of what transcends the merely material, what is spiritual. No amount of scientific calculation can solve the conundrum of spiritual thirst. This is why scientific advances have not and will not eliminate religion.

Neither did the social experiments succeed in ridding humanity of religion. They too succeeded only in redirecting the religious impulse. The communist worldview promised a kind of heaven-on-earth through the elimination of private property. But in practice it yielded an oppressive social regime that stifled much of the human spirit and massacred millions of humans. Other modern ideologies like Nazism and Fascism erected other secular gods—race and nation— only to discover that those deities required their own kinds of unjust human sacrifices and dogmatic superstitions.

Religion itself, then, really can't be the problem, the source of human conflict and injustice. Eliminating religion doesn't resolve social unrest and injustice, nor does it efface the religious yearning in the human heart. Our spiritual experiences open us up to transcendent values whether we want them to or not. We can choose how to respond to those experiences, and we are certainly free to try to explain them away through scientism or some other secular ideology. But the experience is there. And the need to assimilate it, somehow, will continue to impact human history as long as humans are human, if our past is any indicator at all of our future.

An X-Ray of Religion

So we return to the problem of religious differences. Can they be resolved? Is it true that all religions are basically the same, and so their differences can be reconciled simply by more open communication and understanding?

When we reflect on religion in its essence, we can find a satisfying answer to this question.

We have already seen how spirituality and religion intersect. Our human nature leads us to have spiritual experiences, experiences of transcendent values. These give us a satisfaction much deeper than merely material pleasures.

And so we find ourselves thirsting for more. We want to know where those transcendent, spiritual values come from and how to plug into them more fully and more constantly. This is the religious search: Where do we come from? Where are we going? Is there life after death? What will bring me true happiness? What will fulfill the yearning I experience in the very core of my soul when no one else is around and I give myself permission to listen to my heart? Why is there so much evil and suffering in the world, and why do I even care?

These questions flow from the spiritual dimension of our human nature. These questions make sense to every human being. And here we find the first part of our answer to the inquiry as to whether all religions are the same: Yes, all religions are the same, because all religions attempt to answer these most basic questions. If a belief system *doesn't* try to answer these questions, then it is not a religious belief system. Maybe the questions are posed in different ways, but in the end, every religion offers answers to these fundamental questions about the origin, destiny, and meaning of human existence. That's what makes religion religious.

We can go even further. The types of answers religions give are also similar. Religions have dogmas (teachings held as infallibly true) about the three fundamental religious elements.

- First, they have doctrines about the *subject* of religion, the one who engages in religious activity: the human person. Who counts as human? Who is a member of the human community? Where did human beings come from? How must human beings behave in order to flourish?

- Second, they have doctrines about the *object* of religion: divine reality. What does divinity consist of? Is divinity personal or impersonal? Is divinity singular or multiple? Is divinity good, bad, or indifferent?

- Third, religions have doctrines about *the proper way to relate* to divinity, about the behaviors that directly link us to the divine realm. How do we pray? How do we worship? How do we enter into communication and communion with divinity?

These fundamental religious elements provide an x-ray of religion: human beings accepting certain beliefs and engaging in certain actions that bring them into relationship with divinity.

All religions are animated by the same spiritual questions, and they all provide those same three types of answers. This is a common underlying structure that shows how all religions truly are the same: they are all trying to answer the deep questions about meaning that flow from the human spirit. But what about the actual answers they end up giving? Are those answers fundamentally the same as well? That's what we will explore next.

5

A Brief History of Religion

We are still addressing the question of whether all religions are the same. If they are, then being spiritual but not religious makes sense, because the spiritual experience underlying religious trappings is what really matters, not the religious trappings (dogma, ritual, morality) themselves. But if all religions aren't the same, then being spiritual but not religious can't be sufficient, since spiritual experience itself leads us to inquire as to its origin, nature, and destiny, and such an inquiry necessarily enters into the realm of religion.

We have seen that all religions are indeed the same from one perspective: they all try to answer the deepest questions of the human heart, and they all offer the same types of answers. But we can't stop there. We must continue our exploration, seeking to answer another question that is unavoidable for sincere observers of religious phenomena.

Here is that question: if all religions are trying to answer the same questions, do they all give the same answers?

At first glance, it appears that they do not: some believe in multiple gods, others in one God; Jews believe in a Messiah yet to come, Christians in a Messiah who has come already and will come again; animists believe divine spirits inhabit rivers and glades, while Buddha remained silent when asked about divinity; Germanic pagans offered worship through rituals involving human sacrifice, Confucians worship their deceased ancestors, and so on.

Here the elephant parable shows its utility. If that parable were true, all these differences (and many more) would only be *apparent* differences. If religion and spirituality were properly understood, according to the elephant parable, this appearance of difference would dissolve, and religious conflict would no longer be a source of division or strife.

Are these apparently different answers to common religious questions actually all the same? When we look even briefly at the history of religion, and when we consider the different religions respectfully and honestly, it becomes extremely difficult to think that they are.

Religion does have a history. In other words, changes in religion throughout human history make sense. They were not just random inventions; they were linked to the changes of human experience and how that experience affected our perception of self and of the world. And the logic behind those changes reveals the irreconcilable differences between various answers to the religious questions. A brief tour of the history of religion, therefore, can help us continue to unfold the true relationship between spirituality and religion.

For the beginning of this history, we have to go all the way back to the beginnings of the human family.

The science of human origins is still developing. Scientists are still filling in gaps about where and how the first humans (*homo sapiens*) emerged. In recent decades, their painstaking work combining traditional anthropological studies with genetic analysis has opened up new theories about sub-species and interbreeding. But it is fair to say that wherever we find evidence of human behavior like advanced tool-use and the domestication of fire, we also find specific human behaviors that have some sort of religious implication, like burying the dead. Ceremonial burial practices seem to indicate religious sensibility: after death, the material body is treated intentionally and carefully, with hopes that the immaterial soul will somehow benefit.

By the time we have clear evidence of modern humans, we have even clearer evidence of religious activity, like the cave paintings of Lascaux, which seem to indicate the use of religious rituals linked to economic activities like hunting.

In other words, purely anthropological evidence indicates that religion of some form or another has always been with us. Human beings have always been religious. This helps shed light on the peculiar human experience of transcendence. The first humans may not have built museums, but they exhibited the same spiritual capacity for wonder and awe that makes museums make sense. And that spiritual capacity manifested itself in religious activity even in the earliest chapters of human history.

Early Religion

What were the answers that these earliest religious beliefs gave to the basic questions? This is not an easy puzzle to solve since the earliest human communities left sparse evidence behind about their way of life. Some religious historians have attempted to solve the puzzle by studying the religious practices of existing human tribes whose Paleolithic or Mesolithic socio-economic lifestyle seems to mirror that of the more ancient cultures of the first humans. We can describe these first religious practices as early, or primitive religion. As regards specific content (which gods were worshipped, how the worship took place), primitive religion varies as much as the cultures to which they belong. But underlying the specific differences, we find some almost universal characteristics. To understand them, we first have to create a lens through which we can look at human culture in general.

Culture can be described as a common, trans-generational way of life made up of four constitutive elements:

1. Geography: a shared environment where the society dwells, works, and develops.
2. Economy: the way in which that society meets its basic material needs for survival and prosperity.
3. Politics: the habitual way a society makes decisions for the whole group.
4. Ethos: the shared values and beliefs forming the criteria behind those decisions and activities (here is where religion impacts culture).

Paleolithic and Mesolithic cultures were economically pre-agricultural, depending on hunting and gathering rather than sowing and harvesting. As a result, they lived from season to season, their survival extremely vulnerable to climatic or other geographical disruptions. They lived with an acute awareness of the fragility of their existence and its dependence on natural forces outside their control. These factors contributed to keeping their communities relatively small as compared to later Neolithic civilizations like those of Egypt or Mesopotamia. The political structure was usually somewhat democratic, with elders having a strong influence on community decisions and exercising the authority of tribal leaders. These primitive societies vividly illustrate how the four elements of culture closely interact, each one affecting the other.

In this milieu, primitive religion provided the ethos—the shared values and beliefs that gave order to the society—holding the community together. Common characteristics of primitive religion included the following:

- These cultures tend to retain an awareness of a "high god" beyond other spirits. It is notable among these primitive religions especially because this awareness is absent from subsequent religious developments linked to the earliest civilizations.
- They exhibit a more-or-less developed *animism*. This is the attribution of a spiritual soul to plants, inanimate objects, and other natural phenomena (e.g., rivers, mountains, trees, animals). Harnessing the natural powers upon which survival depended, or being protected from those powers, required entering into relationship with the appropriate spirit.
- They exhibit a more-or-less developed *fetishism*. A fetish is an object, usually man-made but sometimes not, serving as a focus of worship and prayerful petition. The

object is a kind of bridge to the spirit world, the realm of the divine. Think of a totem pole, for example.

- They exhibit a more-or-less developed *shamanism*. This is a technique (usually involving music, dance, and other ceremonies) for producing religious ecstasy, an experience in which the shaman somehow enters into the spirit realm and achieves direct contact with divinity. The shaman knows the technique and may also be seen to have a special gift which makes the technique effective. The religious ecstasy can be provoked either for the shaman's personal spiritual advancement or in order to serve the community by entering a state in which spirits can be consulted, questioned, or placated on behalf of the community.

- They make a strong connection between religion and *morality*. This seems to be linked to the awareness of a high god who has standards of behavior that must be respected by humans.

- They show the presence of natural and supernatural *magic*. Magic has to do with accessing hidden power and putting it at the service of an individual or the community. With natural magic, diviners, seers, and healers can accesses hidden powers in the natural world. With supernatural magic, professional experts (sorcerers) will access spiritual powers for good (white magic) or for evil purposes (black magic). Certain magic users (witches, for example) are considered evil in themselves or in partnership with evil spirits only.

In early, primitive religion, the world is teeming with spiritual forces. Everything has a religious significance. The culture itself, the community, cannot be understood apart from its relationship to these forces, but a certain unpredictability and instability characterizes them. In this context, the answers religion gives to existential questions are immediate and practical. Since existence itself is experienced as precarious and dependent on supernatural forces, the distinction between the material world and the spiritual world is hazy at best. Every material reality is charged with spiritual significance, and daily life unfolds with sacred meaning.

It is hard for us post-moderns to imagine what this kind of life would be like. And yet, we can grasp a certain archetypal figure—the wise elder from a primitive tribe—who embodies it. Many a seeker from our own hectic, materialistic world have trekked to distant places still redolent of primitive wisdom hoping to uncover a meaning that seemed to elude them in the sophisticated and alluring environs of New York or London.

Archaic Religion

As the Neolithic Revolution unfolded and those primitive, tribal communities began to practice horticulture (gardening), and eventually agriculture, their relationship to the world around them changed. This in turn affected their ethos and the religious mindset underlying it.

Studying the seasons and the rhythms of nature— for which they began to develop writing in order to keep records—revealed ways to bring their communal life into greater harmony with the natural forces upon which they depended for prosperity. Agricultural techniques allowed them a steadier and more abundant supply of food and other material goods. This in turn created space for the development of specialized labor and classes of experts. These developments laid the groundwork for cities and eventually kingdoms.

In general, this period of material advancement (known as the Neolithic Revolution) coincides with the emergence of the first civilizations. These city-states appear in the traditionally dubbed cradles of civilization (Egypt, Mesopotamia, the Indus River Valley, and northern China) in more or less the same historical period (before the third millennium BC), but independently. In other parts of the world, like Mexico and Peru, archaic civilizations with extremely similar characteristics appeared later in history, and again independently. This seems to indicate a pattern of human development that occurred organically. And just as primitive religions showed common characteristics even among cultures who never had contact with each other, so too the first civilizations showed common religious characteristics. Primitive religion changed into archaic religion just as primitive cultures developed into archaic civilizations.

What are the characteristics of these archaic civilizations? In the first place, by the time advanced urban culture makes its appearance, an educated class is also present. This is the literate and usually priestly class. At this point, the knowledge that enabled advances in agriculture is linked to knowledge of the divine realm: the origin of those forces of nature that permit prosperity (sun, rain, earth, etc.). But the understanding of these forces in an archaic culture differs widely from the understanding of these forces in a primitive culture. In the primitive view, nature was dangerously disordered. The archaic culture, on the other hand, has identified patterns in nature, and their socio-economic reality reflects an ability to harness those forces more regularly and more dependably. The change in religion is linked to this changed understanding of the world. The concept of a high god beyond all other spirits wanes in this period. Ritual—linked to the seasonal rhythms so important for effective agriculture—becomes more important than morality. And a pantheon of gods, hierarchically organized according to the relative importance of the natural forces which these gods controlled, takes the place of the more chaotic and unpredictable animism and fetishism of primitive religion.

This also reflects changes in politics. Generally, the more democratic form of decision-making in primitive cultures transitions to greater centralization. A monarchical organization emerges in which the king is the representative of the particular divinity associated with the community. A more centralized authority allows for more efficient organization of a larger city with diversified economic functions.

The fundamental idea behind archaic civilization, then, is theogamy: a bringing together or synchronization of the material, temporal realm (in which the human community lives and works) and the spiritual, divine realm, understood as the origin of the powers of nature upon which human existence depends. The more fully human society can mirror the rhythms of the unchanging forces of the universe (the seasons, the motion of the stars, the regularity of the solar and lunar cycles, etc.), the more fully human society can share in the harmony and stability exhibited by those forces, or at least that is the hope. The elaborate religious rituals, hierarchical social stratification, and centralized authority become means for achieving that goal.

Archaic civilizations like Mesopotamia, Egypt, and China developed those means, but the goal they sought to achieve by using those means, a perfect theogamy, eluded them. The more prosperous and stable they became, the more they were disrupted by internal conflicts, usually linked to power struggles and external invasions; more primitive peoples envied the wealth of archaic civilizations and invaded them to pillage their riches. This created a cultural mix in which the archaic, agricultural religions clashed with the primitive religions of the invading tribes. This mix eventually led to the emergence of new pantheons in which the divine realm became as confused and conflicted as the human realm.

Here again we see the remarkable connection between spirituality and religion, between a culture's ethos—the values by which it organizes communal life—and its religion. Although archaic civilizations contrasted in so many ways with more primitive cultures, they, too, maintained a strong awareness of the inseparability of spirituality and religion.

That Amazing Century

The mixed cultural environment of the late archaic period became fertile soil for what historians often refer to as the Axial Age. In this period, coinciding with the sixth century BC, religion took its next historical turn.

Experience had shown that theogamy didn't work. Somehow, the exquisite synchronization of social patterns with seasonal rhythms simply didn't produce the hoped for social prosperity and harmony. On the contrary, greater prosperity seemed only to produce greater internal strife and to invite more external invasions. So what was missing? Why did a society built around rituals mirroring the imperturbable harmony of the cosmos not yield an imperturbable harmony in the city-state? New streams of religious thought tried to answer that question.

In China, Confucius recovered a moral underpinning for the archaic system. In India, Buddha's Four Noble Truths and Eightfold Path offered an escape from the endless and apparently pointless cyclical rhythms of earthly life. In the Middle East, Zoroastrianism (perhaps influenced by Judaism) offered a theology of historical progress providing hope for human fulfillment in a future golden age. Taoism, Brahminism, and even the early seeds of Platonism emerged in the same Axial Age, each positing a worldview that offered freedom from the meaninglessness of a merely material world.

Although emerging independently from each other, and organically in regards to their archaic predecessors, these schools of thought all grappled with the same challenge. With them, religion was no longer simply the way to maintain harmony between the divine and the human within the matrix of a cosmos where both were common inhabitants. That had been the vision of primitive and archaic religions. But that vision had not produced what it promised. Now, with the worldview revolutions of the Axial Age, religion became the path out of the changeable, unstable, painful struggle for survival in the material world and into the realm of unchanging spirit; the liberation of the ghost (the sublime human spirit) from the machine (the impermanent material world). The spiritual impulses of the human spirit led in this period to a conviction that the transcendent realm was the true reality, and the material realm was an illusion from which we needed deliverance. This conviction took different forms in different religious developments, but it emerged out of the experience of the more advanced material cultures—the archaic civilizations—in parallel fashion.

This conviction opened a new chapter in religious and cultural history, but the long-term results were a mixture of the old and the new instead of a complete transition to purely contemplative religions. And this only makes sense. The human person is not purely spiritual. We are body and spirit. We experience the impulse to transcendence in and through our material reality. The opposition between our spiritual yearnings and our material needs, in the end, cannot be reconciled by jettisoning either one. Somehow, therefore, the fulfillment of our spiritual longings has to integrate our material dimension. The Judeo-Christian religious ideal (which is also at the origin of Islam) claims to do just that, solving the existential dilemma by uniting bodily and spiritual life. Its personalistic monotheism opens the door to spiritualizing human life without destroying it, to channeling human energy in a way that avoids the purposelessness of materialism and hedonism without denying the reality of the world.

Difficult Doesn't Mean Impossible

This brief tour of the history of religion serves as background for our discussion of the question about whether all religions are the same. It illustrates how all varieties of religious thought seek to answer the same fundamental questions arising in the human heart—and in this sense, we can indeed say that all religions are the same.

But it also illustrates how different religions really do give different answers to those fundamental questions. To affirm that the cosmic realm and the divine realm are actually one and the same (pantheism), leads to religious beliefs, practices, and behaviors different from those linked to faith in a personal creator and savior. To believe in the doctrine of reincarnation and a divinely sanctioned caste-based society leads to concepts of human dignity and social justice fundamentally different from those linked to a doctrine of divine incarnation that reveals all human beings—regardless of social class—as possessing equal dignity. In the former, helping a poor or handicapped person could constitute an offense against the divine mandate and interfere with that person's existential progress. In the latter, *refusing* to help would be the offense and the interference. To believe that human dignity springs solely from belonging to a particular tribe yields far different behaviors from believing in universal human dignity. If the neighboring tribe is less human than mine, I am morally justified in capturing and murdering members of that tribe to make a vicarious, sacrificial offering in atonement for sin, as did the Polynesian head-shrinkers or the Aztec sun-worshippers. If human dignity is universal, however, those types of sacrifices would be morally repugnant.

Although all religions try to answer the same existential questions, they answer them in different ways. Even this brief history of religion makes that undeniably clear. It also makes undeniably clear the practical implications of spirituality; spiritual experience yields changes in mentality that affect how we interact with others and contribute to our communal life. More on that in the following chapter.

So, different religions offer different answers to the same questions about humanity, the world, and divinity. To ignore those differences is to disrespect the adherents of each religion and distort their teachings. We are not blind men touching different parts of the same elephant. We are imperfect men trying to answer questions about the origin, nature, and purpose of the elephant's existence. All religions are the same in their posing the same questions that spring from the spiritual yearnings of our common human nature, but in the answers to those questions, different religions often give very different answers.

But not all the answers are *completely* different. This is why people from different cultures can still interact fruitfully and come to understand each other. This opens up another query. If different religions give different answers, how are we to determine which answers are true? Can there even be religious truth? The short answer to that question is: yes. In fact, the existence of religious truth is a logical necessity.

If religious truth is the answer to our spiritual yearning—our longing for knowledge of and communion with the source of transcendent values—then religious truth must exist. Every other human longing corresponds to a natu-ral, existing object: we get thirsty, and water exists; we get hungry, and food exists; we get tired, and sleep exists; we get short of breath, and air exists. We discover our spiritual longings in the same way that we discover our physical long-ings. We don't invent them; we experience them. And so an existing object—religious truth—must also exist. This is the very structure of the reality we inhabit.

Clearly, our review of religious history shows that satisfy-ing these spiritual longings is more difficult than satisfying the material ones; in other words, religious truth is more dif-ficult to find than a cup of water. But *difficult* doesn't mean *impossible*. To claim that it does would imply that the spir-itual longings themselves are absurd, just as physical thirst would be absurd in a universe without water. If we admit the reality of our spiritual experiences and longings, it is only reasonable to admit that they correspond to something real and existing that will satisfy them. This is what we mean by religious truth. Searching for that truth takes courage, humility, and patience.

The following chapters will try to stir up those virtues by exploring different aspects of this longing and this search. The more clearly we understand our spiritual longings, the better chance we will have of finding their true satisfaction.

6

Spirituality and Politics:
The Search for Community

The brief history of religion offered in the previous chapter illustrated how spiritual experience impacts society. The shared values essential to social living must be anchored somewhere, and unless that anchorage touches transcendence—the unchanging, spiritual realm—it won't be able to provide sufficient stability for a culture to truly flourish.

The Human Being: A Social Animal

But all of that would be irrelevant if individuals could live fulfilling lives on their own. We wouldn't need shared values if each one of us were self-sufficient. In that case, an individual's spiritual experience could stand on its own and each person could freely concoct a personal religious truth without constraint. On the other hand, if human beings are social by nature and not self-sufficient, then the question of shared, transcendent values—to which we have access through our spiritual experiences—cannot be ignored. In that case, the comfort and simplicity of radical individualism is not an option; we must seek those true, lasting values that can construct and preserve a healthy society, and we must find ways to share them. And that is, indeed, the case.

Even introverts need other people. To be human is to exist in relationship with others. This is obvious upon even minimal reflection. We come into being through the spousal relationship of our parents. Unlike other animals, human beings require full-time care for years after birth before we can survive on our own. Family, friendship, belonging, connection, these are fundamental realities of the human experience. Even on a more practical level, economic development requires ongoing coordination of efforts and mutually supportive division of labor. As much as rugged individualism and self-sufficiency have made their way into the pantheon of post-modern ideals, healthy interpersonal relationships continue to be an essential element in any normal person's formula for happiness.

Yet relationships also cause a lot of pain. Families break up. Difficulties at work cause stress. Social injustice leads to revolution, war, and exile. Some might even say that our deepest sufferings are caused by rips in the social fabric of our lives.

The connection with others we yearn for transcends simple physical proximity. We need to share more than the space in which we live. We need to know and be known, to love and to be loved. We need intimacy, the sharing of experiences with people we care about. Our very need for community is imbued with the same longings for transcendence we associate with our spiritual experience and with the religious quest those experiences invite us to undertake. Exploring this dimension of the human condition will shed further light on the intrinsic connection between *spiritual* and *religious*.

The Common Good?

In order to have an environment in which meaningful interpersonal relationships—like family and friendship—can develop in a healthy way, the larger society around us needs to offer a certain modicum of stability and security. This is why every human society we know of has had some sort of legal and political framework. Customs and laws, and a social authority capable of interpreting and applying them, lift a community out of chaos and a jungle-like ethos where the physically stronger members simply do whatever they want to everyone else.

But not just any custom or law will do. A legal framework permitting and encouraging human slavery, for instance, may contribute to a stable social system—as it did in most ancient cultures over the course of thousands of years—but it does so by denying certain people their basic freedoms and rights. This denial comes about through an inadequate response to a religious question: who counts as being human? Who qualifies as a member of our community? To take another example, Nazi Germany excluded entire categories of human beings from participation in German society based solely on race. The German economy flourished under Nazism but at a terrible cost to the social fabric and to millions of individuals, families, and social groups.

The social conditions enabling a society's members, as individuals and groups, to flourish are traditionally described as "the common good." The legal and political framework of a society exists in order to protect and promote the common good, to foster that set of conditions in which the members of a community can thrive. But underlying any conception of the common good is a religious idea about who qualifies as a member of the community.

Many conflictive social issues revolve around that unspoken question. The different positions regarding abortion, for example, are different precisely because of how they define a child still in the mother's womb. Is that a human being? If so, then those children are members of the community and need to be treated as such, just as much as their mothers do. If not, if children only become members of the community once they are born and can survive outside the mother's womb, then they can be treated according to a different standard before birth.

Cogs or Monads?

Promoting the common good, then, requires first of all a clear answer to the question of who belongs to our community, who qualifies as a member of our community. For us, who counts as human? But it also requires answering another fundamental question: what does society owe to its members, and what do its members owe to the society? Beneath that question also lies an often-unspoken assumption about what it means to be human.

Some visions of human nature see individuals as existing solely for the sake of the community. In these cases, individual members are considered cogs in the machine of society.

They can be used and discarded accordingly. This is a collectivist vision of the common good, where the State can dictate how its members must live, overriding individual freedom.

Others envision society existing for the sake of the individuals. In this case, individuals will use society to satisfy their own desires. But what does it mean to "use society"? Society is simply the community of persons united under a set of shared laws, customs, and authority. Society, in other words, is other people. If society exists only to serve my needs, that simply means I can use other people for self-centered ends.

Either of these visions—the collectivist or the ultra-individualist—will lead, if allowed to reach their natural end, to the rule of the strong over the weak: the law of the jungle. The stronger will dominate society either in the name of themselves as individuals or in the name of themselves as guardians of a collective vision.

We can see from this reflection how the question of what it means to be human really matters. How we answer that question will affect how we set up the laws and customs that govern our daily lives. But that question, fundamentally, is a religious question. Human beings didn't invent themselves. Answering the question of our identity, therefore, requires venturing into the transcendent realm: where did we come from and where are we going? Every legal and political system is built upon some answer to this question, whether explicitly or implicitly. Here, choosing to be spiritual but not religious, is not indifferent; the nature of the common good, the social conditions in which we live, will be very different depending on whether we answer this question explicitly or implicitly.

In other words, the phrases "human dignity" and "human rights" don't explain themselves. Their explanation depends on what is meant by "human." And that, in the end, is a religious issue. If human beings are merely random products of a purely material evolution, then concepts like justice and freedom really have no meaning. But if human beings were created with a purpose and an intrinsic, lasting spiritual value, then concepts like justice and freedom may indeed be clues to an objectively fruitful pursuit of the common good.

The mere recognition of both our individuality and our need for others indicates where the religious truth about human identity must reside. We know we are not just cogs in a machine. But we also know we have a common, relational nature with our fellow human beings—we need meaningful relationships with others to live our own life to the fullest; simply using them, in the ultra-individualist way, leaves our need for authentic, mutually enriching interpersonal relationships unfulfilled. Somehow, being human means having an intrinsic, individual dignity that is inherently open and in need of completion through meaningful contact with others. The common good, then, needs to respect both of these dimensions. If it doesn't, it won't be worthy of human beings, and it won't create the conditions necessary for us to flourish as individuals created to live and thrive in relationship with others.

But which human beings are we talking about? Is it obvious who counts as a member of the human family? Do some human beings have rights that others don't have? The question of human rights touches directly on our innate need for community. A right is the moral capacity to demand from others one's due, and making demands on each other profoundly affects the quality of social experience. If society makes too many demands on me, I will live a frustrated life. A society making too few demands on its members may undermine the stability and security needed for the common good, creating social conditions ripe for the emergence of the law of the jungle. The question of rights, then, is critical; what should members of a society expect from each other in their shared pursuit of the common good? And it is impossible to answer this question without venturing—explicitly or implicitly—into the spiritual-religious realm.

Legal Rights

Basically, rights come in three different types. The most obvious type of right is a civil or legal right. The legitimate authority of the society (the *civitas* in the ancient Latin term) confers civil rights through its laws or customs—the shared standards of behavior that make a common way of life possible in the first place. When the light turns green, I have a right to drive through the intersection. That right enables me to expect other drivers to let me do that by stopping at their red light. If someone ignores their red light and crashes into me, I can expect them to make recompense for damages. And if they refuse, I can defend my civil rights by taking them to court.

Nothing in my human nature, *per se*, indicates that a green light authorizes me to drive forward. This right, in other words, doesn't flow directly from my being human. It flows indirectly because human nature requires us to live in society with other human beings, and society requires stability and security, and traffic laws facilitate stability and security when it comes to travel and transportation. But the specific traffic laws themselves are conceived, written, and promulgated solely by the governing authority of the society. They are invented by human creativity, not discovered in the depths of human nature. This is the realm of civil or legal rights, rights conferred by social authority to promote and protect the common good.

Notice that any civil rights also correspond to a civil duty. I have a right to drive through a green light. I also have a duty to stop at a red light. We might even say that I have a duty to drive through the green light; if I don't, I will obstruct the flow of traffic, violating (in a sense) the civil rights of the folks behind me on the road, maybe even creating traffic chaos or causing an accident. Rights are like that. Since they have to do with mutual expectations regarding the behavior of members of a community, every right has a corresponding duty. Any other understanding of rights violates the rich bi-dimensional character of the human person as an independent individual necessarily living in an interdependent community.

Contractual Rights

Civil rights are similar to a second type of right, contractual rights. When two parties make a contractual agreement, they confer rights and duties on each other. If I sign a contract with a lawn care company, I accrue a right to receive their lawn services, and they accrue a right to be paid for those services. Here again, each right comes with a corresponding duty. I have a duty to make payment for their services; they have duty to provide the promised services. If either of us fails in our duty, we violate the other's contractual right. In that case, they could appeal to the legitimate authority (for example, filing a lawsuit) for fair compensation.

Contractual rites also flow from human creativity. Contracts are concocted by human beings, not discovered in the nature of things. But the rights they confer are real. We all agree that signing a contract and then reneging on that contract without due cause is, simply put, unfair.

The concept of fairness undergirds this whole discussion of rights. It brings us back to the definition of a right: the moral capacity to demand from others one's due. When we speak of a moral capacity, we are referring to the power not of physical coercion but of *spiritual* coercion. This brings us back to the spiritual dimension of our human need for community; a society must be able to protect what is fair, and that is a spiritual reality.

In other words, this moral capacity to demand one's due can be challenged. If someone runs a red light and totals my car, they may try to drive away or claim that I was the one who ran the red light. It is for situations like this that every human society has some sort of justice system. Violated rights must be fairly defended, and unfulfilled duties can lead to social disintegration. Without a proper authority to appeal to in these cases, we once again revert to the law of the jungle. If I can't call the police to intervene after a hit-and-run, I may have to take the law into my own hands to put things right. But if everyone does that, eventually the strongest person or group (the one capable of the most effective violence) will end up being the arbiter of everyone's rights. Their whim becomes the only law. This is evident in feudal societies and the institutionalized injustice that goes along with them.

But where is the concept of fairness and the moral capacity to demand what is fairly one's own rooted? Both legal and contractual rights seem to presuppose the concept of fairness. This becomes clear if we ask whether we can have an unfair contract, or an unfair civil law. The answer to both those questions is certainly yes.

Think, for example, of how poor people can be exploited by employers. A poor person is concerned about day-to-day sustenance. With few options for how to make a living, the poor may become desperate. Simply in order to scrape by, they may be willing to work inhumane hours under inhumane conditions for mere survival wages. A greedy employer may be willing draw up an unfair contract to take advantage of such a person. Both parties agree to the contract, but the contract itself unreasonably privileges one party to the extent that the other party will actually damage themselves in fulfilling it, at least in the long run. The movements for workers unions in the aftermath of the industrial revolution grew out of just such conditions. That's an example of an unfair contract.

For an unfair civil law, we only have to look at the example of the racial segregation laws prior to the US Civil Rights movement in the mid-twentieth century. According to legitimately passed laws at the time, it was civilly justified to marginalize an entire race of people. White Americans

enjoyed the freedom to participate fully in all the opportunities and privileges of the civil society at the time, and
black Americans did not. Equally egregious laws have been
legitimately passed and enforced throughout history: When
the law allows me to take my neighbors' property simply
because my neighbor is of a different race or creed, that law
is clearly unfair. The rights and duties it confers are unfair.
Just because something is legal, in other words, doesn't mean
it is right.

Natural Rights

This sense of fairness—a spiritual, transcendent value—pre-
supposed by legal and contractual rights flows from a third
type of right. People refer to this third category in various
ways: human rights, fundamental rights, basic rights, natural
rights, et cetera. Too often, conversations about rights fail to
make the distinction between legal (civil), contractual, and
fundamental human rights. This contributes to unnecessary
confusion and strife in public (as well as private) discourse.
The resulting conflicts drain social energy. If we can clarify
the distinction by digging into what this third type of right
really is, we can avoid useless conflicts and engage in more
meaningful and constructive exchanges.

A fundamental human right still fits under our general
definition of rights: a moral capacity to demand from others
one's due. But "one's due" comes from a different place. For
legal rights, one's due comes from laws made by legitimate
authority. For contractual rights, one's due comes from the
agreement between the parties who sign onto the contract.

For natural rights, one's due flows from our human nature itself. A natural right, then, doesn't change. This is why contracts and laws can be unfair or unjust. When human constructs like contracts and laws contradict what is naturally due to a human being (natural rights), they violate a deeper law, what is commonly called the natural law.

And so, Nazi leaders could be convicted of "crimes against humanity," of engaging in activities legal under civil law but contrary to natural law, to what is due to every human being simply because they are human. We don't invent this natural law the way we invent contracts and civil legal systems. Rather, we discover it written into our human nature. It is prior to any human construct and therefore serves as a standard by which civil laws and contracts can be evaluated. Any civil law that dehumanizes a particular group of human beings, as did the Nazi laws or the racial laws prior to the civil rights movement, contradicts the common good precisely because it distorts the truth about human communities.

But why is human nature unchangeable, and why should we respect the law we find inscribed within human nature? These are critical questions. If we believe that human nature itself is only material, and so malleable as all other material realities, or if we believe that what is due to human beings just because they are human is only optional, not obligatory, then the underlying foundation of spiritual concepts like "fair" and "just" disappears. They can be redefined by whoever is clever or powerful enough to impose their own opinion on others through civil laws, contracts, or the mere use of force.

Up to a certain point, common sense is sufficient to understand fairness. But only up to a certain point. We can only fully understand the unchangeability of human nature and the moral obligation to respect what is due to human beings simply because they are human when we move into the realm of religion. If something about human beings demands a different kind of respect than spiders and squirrels, for example, it flows from our origin, nature, and destiny. And we made none of those. The questions of ultimate origin, nature, and destiny are religious questions that flow from our spiritual experience (the experience of something being "unfair" is a kind of spiritual experience). And since different religions give different answers to these questions, we can clearly see that religious belief can never simply remain a private concern. Religion by its very nature has a spiritual dimension impacting the very fabric of social living. We can never build or experience authentic community unless we adopt, implicitly or explicitly, some kind of religious viewpoint. Here again, we see that spiritual is not enough; our experience of transcendent values leads us inexorably toward religion.

What Do We Really Mean by Human Dignity?

The quality differentiating human beings from squirrels and spiders is generally referred to as human dignity. Human rights—what is due to all human beings simply because of their humanity—flow from this human dignity.

Some worldviews deny the existence of human dignity at all. Pantheism, for example, sees the whole cosmos as one divine being, and the apparent differences between things are just an illusion. Certain environmentalists, to take another example, see human beings as a kind of cancer slowly destroying the non-human world, which alone has dignity worth respecting.

Yet, denying human dignity altogether leads once again to the law of the jungle. Without a shared dignity, human beings have no natural rights, and without natural rights, concepts like fairness and justice lose their meaning. In other words, what we consider due to every human being simply because of their human nature depends on how we conceive of that nature.

We should point out once again the connection between rights and duties. Just as a civil right or a contractual right always goes with a civil or contractual duty, so too a natural right goes with a natural duty. If human beings have a right to work, they also have a duty to work. In that case, neglecting that duty would be an affront against one's own dignity, as well as a detriment to the community.

Many social issues facing post-modern society touch directly on this hidden but crucial question of human dignity. Legalizing assisted suicide, for example, implicitly affirms that human beings who no longer feel like living, or whose caretakers no longer want to take care of them, lose their right to life and their corresponding duty to take care of themselves. That point of view implicitly claims that such persons are no longer truly human. Their human dignity has somehow evaporated because of the suffering they are undergoing. Therefore other members of the society no longer need to show them the respect due to human beings.

Their suffering has separated them from the community. Underlying this line of reasoning is an unstated religious point of view: the meaning of life depends on being able to avoid a certain threshold of suffering.

Few proponents of legalizing assisted suicide realize that their position implies a religious stance, but when we pause to reflect on it, that's exactly what we find.

Other hot-button social issues have similar profiles. Pro-abortion advocates, for example, implicitly deny the human dignity of an unborn baby while they defend the mother's human dignity. In essence, they claim that an unborn baby is not human. But behind that explicit denial is an implicit affirmation that human nature depends on a baby's viability outside the womb. Such viability varies greatly depending upon what kind of medical attention is available. Following that line of reasoning to its logical consequences leads us to the conclusion that human nature really is changeable, and so human dignity and human rights are too. This opens the door once again to the clever and the powerful creating an arbitrary standard for what "one's due" really is, which is just another version of the law of the jungle.

The most fundamental question behind our spiritual search for authentic community and the common good is, therefore, a religious question: Who counts as a human being? And since different religious viewpoints give different answers to that question, religion must not be relegated to the private sphere; in other words, it must not be reduced to subjective spiritual experiences. That would create an ethos-vacuum that will eventually be filled with some kind of ideology proposed by the strong at the expense of the weak. Settling for *spiritual but not religious* has dire consequences for social living.

Solidarity and Subsidiarity

The stability and security of a just society depends on more than simply laws, however. Unfair civil laws and customs damage the common good, but fair laws and customs don't automatically lead to social flourishing. The individuals and members of a society must be committed to respecting each other's rights and fulfilling one's duties. Since we all need society in order to become fully ourselves, we all must be committed to working for the good of others by supporting and nourishing the social fabric. This firm attitude, this commitment to be a responsible member of the community in which one lives, is sometimes referred to as the virtue or principle of solidarity.

Solidarity reflects the two sides of human freedom. On the one hand, human persons deserve to be free *from* oppression and want. But on the other hand, human persons experience their innate freedom as a call *to* something, to develop themselves and the society around them. This is another reflection of the two sides of human dignity: that every right has a corresponding duty. We have a right to live freely in society with others, but that right goes along with a duty to contribute to that society. When everyone just clamors for their rights while ignoring their duties, the social fabric is weakened. If we expect the government to give us everything we need for a flourishing life, we forfeit our own dignity, our own duty to make something of ourselves and to make our own unique contribution to the community around us. This is why so-called welfare states sap social vitality; the energy and creativity of solidarity is stifled by a nanny state that doesn't trust its own citizens to be fully engaged in pursuing and protecting the common good.

Just as members of a society have a responsibility to contribute to the common good—to live the virtue of solidarity—so the social authority has a certain responsibility toward those members. Making, enforcing, and adjudicating wise and just laws is the primary responsibility. But at times the authority also needs to come to the aid of members of the society who are in trouble and unable to fulfill their own duties. The most obvious example is in the case of natural disasters. In the wake of a hurricane, for example, communities may need special help recovering. When the government sends in the national guard to help a community get back on its feet, it is offering subsidiarity as a complement to solidarity. Subsidiarity is the principle guiding a social authority not to interfere in or take over the legitimate interior activities of a society's members, but to coordinate those activities (through the making, executing, and adjudicating of wise and just laws—think of traffic laws, for example) and helping its members when they are in need and unable to help themselves. Helping members in need can happen in many ways. Unemployment benefits would be a direct way of helping someone in need. Tax incentives for supporting not-for-profit service organizations would be an indirect way of helping.

Together, the principles of solidarity (each member being committed to supporting the common good) and subsidiarity (the social authority coordinating and helping, but without stifling the creativity and vitality of the individuals and groups) reflect the dual nature of the common good. Because we as human beings are social by nature, what is truly good for us as individuals will also be truly good for the community in which we live, and vice versa. Neglecting either side of the equation leads to imbalance of one sort or another. Either the community fails to adequately respect the individual or the individual fails to contribute sufficiently to the community.

A Spirituality of Social Living

Reflecting on how these two principles contribute to promoting the common good brings us back once again to the connection between spirituality and religion. People are not merely machines. They cannot be programmed to create a perfectly ordered hive. Good laws are not enough for a good society. The members of the society themselves must choose to have a disposition of good will toward others. This disposition cannot flow simply from self-interest, because promoting the common good will always require some self-sacrifice—we cannot enjoy security on the roads if we are not willing to stop at red lights and concede the right of way at stop signs.

Truly seeking the good of society through living out the principles of subsidiarity and solidarity implies a vision of what a truly good society looks like, which in turn implies a vision of what human nature is like, and that, as we have seen, necessarily includes some kind of answers to the religious questions of origin, purpose, and destiny.

Simply put, behind social living lies a spirituality of life with religious implications. We cannot engage in politics without touching on religion, whether consciously or not. We cannot build community without choosing which transcendent values to recognize and protect. Our search for community necessarily includes a search for communion, for what is common to each and therefore treasured by all.

The search for meaning in a material world includes building a healthy society, and a healthy society depends upon a spiritual vision that takes a religious stand, either knowingly or unknowingly. Politics is not just about politics, just as economy is not just about economy. Undergirding all of our common life is an ethos, whether we want to admit it or not.

St. George in a niche with a relief of St. George slaying the dragon below (marble) (see also 55431 & 87899), Donatello, (c.1386-1466) / Museo Nazionale del Barg- ello, Florence, Tuscany, Italy / Bridgeman Images

The Talking Oak, 1857 (oil on canvas), Egley, William Maw (1826-1916) / Detroit Institute of Arts, USA / Founders Society Purchase, R.H. Tannahill Foundation fund / Bridgeman Images

The Devout Childhood of Saint Elizabeth of Hungary, 1852 (oil on canvas), Collins, Charles Alston (1828-73) / Private Collection / Photo © The Maas Gallery, London / Bridgeman Images

Celadon and Amelia, 1793 (oil on canvas), Hamilton, William (1751-1801), Detroit Institute of Arts, USA. Photograph by Sailko (2016), Public domain via Wikiemedia Commons.

Marguerite Leaving Church, 1838 (oil on canvas), Scheffer, Ary (1795-1858) / Detroit Institute of Arts, USA / Founders Society Purchase, Robert H. Tannahill Foundation Fund / Bridgeman Images

Above: The Nightmare, 1781 (oil on canvas), Fuseli, Henry (Fussli, Johann Hein-rich) (1741-1825) / Detroit Institute of Arts, USA / Founders Society Purchase with funds from Mr. and Mrs. Bert L. Smokler and Mr. and Mrs. Lawrence A. Fleischmanf / Bridgeman Images

Right: Cotopaxi, 1862 (oil on canvas), Church, Frederic Edwin (1826-1900) / Detroit Institute of Arts, USA / Founders Society Purchase / Bridgeman Images

Interior of St. Peter's Basilica in Rome, Italy. Photo by grafalex/Shutterstock.

7

Spirituality and Entertainment: The Search for a Happy Ending

Telling stories is a human thing, and so we know it is also a spiritual thing. We don't find frogs gathered around listening to frog tales, or centipedes listening to centipede tales, or dogs eagerly looking forward to the next *Star Wars* episode. But we do find people everywhere and of every historical period telling and listening to stories.

Since recorded history began (and therefore, we can fairly extrapolate, since *before* recorded human history began), human beings have used stories as a way to understand themselves and the world around them. Myths and their accompanying rituals wove story into religion. Epic sagas passed on orally for generations helped educate peoples in their language, identity, and creeds. Think of Gilgamesh and Odysseus, or the plays of Sophocles written as offerings for religious festivals. Something about stories is spiritual. Something about entertainment expresses and shapes our search for meaning and transcendence.

I remember conversing once with a Hollywoodian about what makes for a good movie. He worked in a small production company as a script filterer. He would read all the submitted screenplays and recommend some of them for review by folks higher up on the decision-making chain. I asked him how he could tell if a screenplay was good. He enthusiastically explained concepts like story arc, suspense, and character development. He told me all about the technicalities of good storytelling. And then I asked him, "What about the message?" He frowned back at me, puzzled. *What did I mean? What does message have to do with story?* That's when I realized that not everyone who loved stories was aware of the spirituality behind them. If we do become aware of it, our search for meaning in this material world will have a much better chance of success. Elevating that awareness is what this chapter is all about.

The Mystery of Entertainment

Stories are entertaining because of the emotional charge and vicarious experience they provide. We identify with the characters in the story. We project ourselves into them. Through that identification, we share in the emotions they feel as their adventure unfolds. And in a well-told story, the protagonist goes through an intense emotional journey—that's what "drama" is all about. Feeling those emotions through another character is entertaining because emotions make us feel alive and experiencing them vicariously is safe.

A wild adventure is also entertaining because we thirst to engage with reality, to experience things and discover things and learn things. The human spirit is inquisitive. A good story can take us to new places, expose us to new situations and challenges, and introduce us to new people, satisfying, once again vicariously, our desire for more engagement with reality. The better a story is, the deeper the emotional charge it gives us and the richer the span of experience it gives us.

Just on that level, this whole dynamic reflects a certain spirituality. The ability to follow a story with our mind and imagination presupposes a certain type of consciousness, a certain type of intelligence and self-awareness not limited to the materiality of the here-and-now. We are carried away from the merely material confines of our living room or favorite chair by the words, images, and sounds being used to tell us the story. The mere acts of storytelling and story-hearing are intrinsically spiritual. Anyone who enjoys a good story is already dipping into a spiritual experience.

Another level of spirituality in story has to do with what we learn through the fresh experience it gives us. The story-teller fills the story with information, and in the context of a gripping plot, that information tends to stick with us. A story taking place in a foreign culture instructs us, to some extent, about that culture. A story about space travel may instruct us about the scientific conundrums involved in space travel. This learning is part of the vicarious experiencing, but it doesn't end when the story ends. It stays with us. We are enriched in our minds even though, *materially* speaking, we are the same before and after hearing the story.

The Mystery of Inspiration

But it goes even deeper. Underneath all the vicarious emotion and engagement, we find something that not only entertains but also inspires. When we identify with the hero of a story, we not only feel what the hero feels and experience what the hero experiences but are also filled with hope. Maybe, we think either consciously or not, if we can somehow imitate in our own lives the choices made by the hero in the story, we will also be able to experience for real (not just vicariously) the hero's sense of achievement and satisfaction. We come to associate the emotional experience given to us by the story with the behavior that drove the hero's action and success. And certain values guided that behavior. If we adopt those values, then our own behavior may follow the same pattern and lead us to incarnate the hero's journey in our own lives.

That is how a good story can inspire us. It gives us hope. By following the hero's example, our own lives can reflect the greatness we found so satisfying in the hero's achievement.

And here is where the message comes in. Every story has a message. Every story shows heroic choices being rewarded and villainous choices being punished. The heroic choices stir up positive emotions. And so a story tells us that those choices, and the values motivating them, are the right ones, the ones that will help enhance our life experience. Those choices and values will lead to victory, to satisfaction, to the vitality of success exhibited by the hero. What is rewarded in the story reveals the message of the story. Good Cinderella eventually discovers love and gets to marry the prince; her evil step sisters do not. Therefore, the story tells us, we should avoid being selfish and abusive like the evil step sisters and choose to be obedient, hopeful, and humble like Cinderella.

If the hero of a story only finds inner peace by resisting religious dogma and ending a loved one's life through euthanasia, the message clearly promotes euthanasia and warns against religion. Every drama—because making choices based on certain values is what leads to the resolution of the conflict—always contains some kind of message.

Even in a tragedy, the heroic self-sacrifice of a hero stirs up strong emotions and communicates a message. Romeo and Juliet don't live happily ever after, but their love is so powerful that it ends a violent family feud; romantic love, the story tells us, should never be denied. Faust makes a deal with the devil that wreaks havoc in people's lives the way a stone thrown into water sends ripples across the whole pond. And so, the message goes, we want to avoid responding to our own frustrations the way Faust responded to his.

A Social Impact

A single story may have a lasting impact on us if the story is powerful enough, the message clear enough, and we are in a particularly formative moment or season of life. But the real lasting impact usually comes from a message repeated in various stories. And the impact extends beyond merely an individual when the stories are effectively shared with a whole community.

Thus the tales of chivalry that emerged in the early Middle Ages ended up having a profound impact on the transformation of a pagan, warrior-based culture in which "might made right" into a Christian culture where might was only seen as right when it was put at the service of those who could not defend themselves.

This also explains why totalitarian governments so quickly monopolize not only the society's educational system but also their entertainment industry. Both Hitler and Stalin showed keen interest in mobilizing the storytelling machinery of their countries for the sake of promoting their ideology. Shared stories influence shared values. A culture's ethos is always connected to the worldview at work in its stories. If we understand the Iliad and the Odyssey, we understand ancient Greece.

A Musical Interlude

Music, another form of entertainment, is similar to story but not exactly the same. In story, we identify with the characters and vicariously share their emotions and experiences. The message inspires us to follow their example—to make choices like theirs, behaving according to their values—through the intensity of those vicarious emotions and experiences.

Music also stirs our emotions and provides inspiration but in a slightly different way. Although lyrics often tell a story or communicate a message, the emotional impact actually flows from the melodies, rhythms, and harmonies unique to the musical medium. The music itself stirs the emotions directly. This is why, for example, a Gregorian chant album can sell millions of units even to people who have no idea how to understand Latin; the soothing and calming mood of order, peace, and simplicity is transmitted primarily through the chant's musical characteristics.

The experience can go deeper than mere emotion when a listener also pays attention to the lyrics because then the values expressed by the words can be associated with the emotions felt by the listener. If we like the emotions, we may be more easily convinced by the values. But the emotional stimulus at the core of the entertainment value, the heart of music's power, is in the sound, not the words.

More complex music bridges the emotions and the mind without resorting to lyrics. Classical music is the exemplar here. The complexity of the structure engages the mind while the beauty of the sounds stimulates the emotions. This is the secret to the perennial power of the classical repertoire. Since we as human beings are not pure emotion, music that brings together intellect and feeling is more fully human, more satisfying, once we learn to listen to it and if we are not overly attached to raw emotion, which is an attachment promoted by certain forms of music that violently stimulate basic emotional experiences and isolate them from rational reflection.

This is why music as well as story has always been a part of religious piety. Music helps engage the emotions in the act of worship. In early religion, ritual shamanic dances and the music associated with them stimulated such intense emotional experiences that they elevated the shaman to an ecstatic state, a state beyond the ordinary materiality of daily life, a state conducive to conversation with the spiritual realm.

Entertainment and Religion

Here we see an interesting variation on the relationship between entertainment and religion. On the one hand, the inspiration provided by a powerful story can move us to accept values and adopt behaviors in harmony with particular religious beliefs, with a particular ethos or worldview. Those behaviors and values in turn promise to increase a believer's communion with divinity, the source of meaning and fulfillment. On the other hand, music and other ritual practices involving the body (like dance or yoga) are offered in some religious contexts as a stimulus to an ecstatic experience redolent of that same communion with the divine. Both cases exemplify the spirituality of entertainment, but they actually indicate contrasting approaches to experiencing the transcendent.

The ritual-as-stimulus approach implies that authentic religious experience can be manufactured. This comes close to superstition in that it offers the human person a technique for touching the divine. But if divinity is reachable merely by a technique—a form of meditation or ritual, for example, focusing on bodily and emotional experience while minimizing the role of the intellect—then the relationship between the human heart and the divine reality is one-directional. There is nothing interpersonal about it. In fact, in some types of transcendental meditation, the very goal of the ritual prayer is to escape from one's personhood and dissolve into a kind of divine ether.

The story-as-inspiration type approach, on the other hand, highlights the human capacity for knowing and choosing.

The proper exercise of our personal freedom becomes the avenue to interpersonal communion with the divine. The emotional experience flowing from that communion is a kind of bonus, but the meaning that comes from the relationship goes deeper than a bodily and emotional ecstatic experience. Just as human friendships are built on a substratum of knowledge and goodwill that can weather seasons of emotional dryness as well as seasons of emotional intensity, the interpersonal approach to communion with the divine can endure and inform one's daily life independently of emotional states. Prayer in this context is not a technique for manufacturing an ecstatic experience but a true dialogue between persons. Thus, once again, we see that different religions propose different paths and different destinies.

In both cases, however, the gratifying emotional experience we associate with entertainment naturally opens us up to the spiritual realm, the realm of transcendence, even though not every piece of entertainment is explicitly transcendent in its form or content. And so the question about meaning and fulfillment must grapple with entertainment, and entertainers must learn to be aware of the impact made by the utilization of their gifts.

Living Happily Ever After

Yet another spiritual dimension of story emerges when we reflect on the power of the famous phrase, "and they lived happily ever after." It is a good ending to a good story, just as "Once upon a time . . ." is a good beginning to a good story.

We naturally hope for a happy ending. This seems obvious. But is it?

In some of the world-denying religious traditions, any hope for happiness or fulfillment is considered an illusion. After all, the world in which we live doesn't really seem to be going anywhere. Rather, the weather patterns go through an apparently endless cycle of repetitive seasons, and the motion of the sun, moon, and stars also cycle through patterns that seem to repeat themselves endlessly. Even the rhythms of life and death seem to point to an eternal return of the same: a tree grows in the soil, then eventually dies, collapses, and decays back into the soil, which then produces another tree. The idea of progress, the idea that we actually may be coming from somewhere and going somewhere purposeful is not necessarily self-evident.

Yet, that idea gives story its power. Something is different in the lives of the characters at the end of the story. Somehow, their experience of the ups and downs of the drama, their suffering and overcoming the obstacles and meeting the challenges, leads them to a better place, either literally, symbolically, or both. And that resonates with us. Why?

Somewhere deep within us, we discover a realization that things are not the way they should be. We find ourselves in a situation, a world, where we know we belong, and yet we yearn for more. Unlike squirrels and spiders, which are content to hoard their nuts and spin their webs, the human spirit always strives for more. We have a sense that the future can, somehow, be better than the present. We have a hope in future progress even while we recognize the imperfections of our broken present. Somehow, this dichotomy must be reconciled for us to experience interior peace. Many of humanity's great stories reconcile it through presenting a happy ending to a troubled journey. They offer a paradigm of hope to pilgrims still on their way.

The Mystery of Sports

This is one reason why sports—or games of any kind, even video games—can be so entertaining. A game provides many elements that good stories provide: characters, conflict, clear challenges, opportunities to try again, and, above all, an ending.

A game is a lifetime in miniature. It has a beginning, filled with uncertainty and promise. It unfolds gradually and within the scope of some predetermined conditions (the rules of the game), just as our own lives have predetermined conditions we simply must accept (where we are born, what our parents are like, etc.). Then, a sporting contest unfolds unpredictably—no two football games have ever followed the exact same sequence of plays; no two baseball games have ever followed the exact same sequence of pitches and pop flies. Just so, our lives take twists and turns we never would have anticipated. Challenges and opportunities present themselves one after another, and we must respond as best we can. Then, finally, the game comes to an end. Someone wins, someone loses.

And this is the big difference. While we are still living, the game of life is still in progress. We are in the middle of it, just as players at halftime are still in the middle of the drama. When we watch a game from start to finish, we experience the *full* drama, the beginning, the middle, *and the end.* In our own lives, we don't get that. We are always in the middle. And so sports offer us the same kind of vicarious fulfillment offered by other types of stories. The game resolves. The season ends. The experience of spectator sports mirrors the experience of life, but it allows us a temporary escape from the actual drama of our lives (which is unresolved) because the whole drama of the game is played out in front of us to its final conclusion. And it nourishes our hope because we vicariously experience the resolution of an ending that we never get to experience ourselves, at least definitely, here in the realm of time and space. The happy ending of a good story, and the satisfying resolution of a good game, inspire us to aspire to our own happy ending and our own good resolution.

Sports, like stories, have been entertaining human communities since the dawn of history. And, also like stories, athletic contests have often been associated with religious festivals. In ancient Greece, the Olympic Games had their origin as a festival in honor of the gods of Olympus. And this too makes sense. Besides the impressive display of physical prowess and excellence sports have always emphasized, and the training in virtue and combat skill they entail, the drama of competition appeals to our innate yearning for something more, our hope that if we exert ourselves, we may be able to improve ourselves and fulfill our deepest desires. This spiritual longing, evidenced by the perennial appeal of stories and sport, opens our hearts to the transcendent, lifts us above the merely material, and stirs in our souls the same thirst for transcendence present in dynamism of religion.

Our Story

Becoming more conscious of the spirituality behind entertainment, and especially of the spiritual values at work in the types of entertainment that appeal to us personally, is one way to continue moving forward in our search for meaning. If our entertainment choices are superficial or unconscious, we may end up lulling our spirits to sleep with petty distractions, or even with increasingly self-destructive vices. On the other hand, if we become more aware of the spirituality intrinsic to entertainment, we can begin to reflect on our experience and find in it some clues to what will bring us the lasting satisfaction we truly long for.

I remember well how my own journey into Catholicism included a growing fascination with the story of the Catholic Church as a whole, as well as the stories of its most exemplary members, the saints. A university semester in Europe brought me into personal contact with Catholic cultural artifacts (like churches, shrines, monasteries, and works of art) that told many stories, all of which fit together into one mega-story of salvation that reached back to the dawn of human history.

During that same year abroad, I participated in a study program in Krakow, Poland, which at the time was under the political sway of the officially atheistic Soviet Union. And there I witnessed how the story of the Catholic Church and its heroic men and women wasn't just something that belonged to the past; it was still unfolding. Hope for liberation from communist oppression was being nourished—intentionally, powerfully, courageously—by the Catholic faith, the Catholic faithful behind the Iron Curtain, and the Polish pope. Present events would eventually be commemorated in future shrines and artifacts that continued to tell the story I was reading in the previous shrines and artifacts. It was all part of the same grand story.

It began to occur to me that I myself could choose to enter into this amazing story if I were to enter that Church. The prospect of becoming part of that story—so beautiful, so meaningful, so mysterious—tugged at the very depths of my heart and helped change the direction of my life.

What stories move you? What is the spirituality behind them? What kind of story do you want your own life to tell? These are questions that can help us move forward in our quest for transcendence and bring us closer to the meaning we yearn for.

8

Spirituality and Suffering: The Search for Safety and Healing

In discussing the dynamism of hope, we mentioned the incompleteness and brokenness of the world in which we live, the sense we have that the world is not as it should be. Tsunamis shouldn't devastate thousands of human communities. Cancer shouldn't kill five-year-old children. The Nazis should never have perpetrated the Holocaust. Priests shouldn't sexually abuse the very people they are called to serve. People shouldn't purposely crash airplanes into sky scrapers.

As much as we experience these and other realities as wrong, they still happen. Why? What is the meaning of such horrors? This question, too, arises in the human heart and challenges us to find an answer.

By its very nature, the question of human suffering is a spiritual question. Suffering is part of our material existence. If we were merely material beings, why would we question it? Why don't we simply accept it the way we accept the existence of the earth beneath our feet and the sky above our heads? At the root of our dissatisfaction with suffering is something immaterial, something spiritual. Any authentic spirituality must at some point come to grips with the problem of suffering, and this, too, involves opening the door to religious questions.

Physical Evil

The most obvious type of suffering is the kind caused by impersonal forces—disease and natural disasters. The very world in which we live seems at times to rise up against us. The very environment we depend on for our existence seems to become our enemy.

James Thomson's book length poem *The Seasons* presents this apparent absurdity in his stanzas on summer. He describes a scene whose pathos has captured the imagination of multiple artists through the centuries.

Celdon and Amelia were young lovers, innocent and true, a perfect match living a perfect fidelity and full of promise:

> And yet not always on the guilty head
> Descends the fated flash. Young Celadon
> And his Amelia were a matchless pair;
> With equal virtue form'd, and equal grace.
> The same, distinguish'd by their sex alone:
> Her the mild lustre of the blooming morn,
> And his the radiance of the risen day.

They were walking in the woods together in the summer when a violent storm caught them unawares. The thunder and lightning shook the forest so severely that the maiden Amelia collapsed into Celadon's embrace:

> Thus pass'd their life, a clear united stream,

By care unruffled; till in evil hour
The tempest caught them on the tender walk,
Heedless how far. Her breast presageful heav'd
Unwonted sighs, and stealing oft a look
Of the big gloom, on Celadon her eye
Fell tearful, wetting her disorder'd cheek.

Celadon holds her surely and comforts her as the storm
rages on. But the shock of the blast is too much for her, and
contrary to every expectation and all reason, she dies in her
lover's arms:

From his void embrace,
(Mysterious heaven!) that moment, in a heap
Of pallid ashes fell the beauteous maid.
But who can paint the lover, as he stood,
Struck by severe amazement, hating life,
Speechless, and fix'd in all the death of woe!

William Hamilton's 1793 painting of the scene illustrates
the drastic contrast between this young couple's limitless
possibilities and their horrific termination at the instigation
of the storm. The forest is shown racked by wind and rain,
the trees bending and writhing darkly, menacingly around
the two figures. They, on the other hand, are all brightness
and purity, he dressed in gold and she in shining white.
Their every feature breathes out life, vitality, goodness, and
promise. Except that his strong arms now envelop a pallid,
lifeless corpse. They had done everything right, preserving
their innocence, living in the purest and most generous love
and friendship, and they shared perfect prospects and hopes

for a glorious future. All of that is now gone, shattered, violently and mindlessly ended before it even began. We can see in Celadon's face the perplexed and helpless rage of someone whose life will be forever scarred by this senseless loss.

A spirituality that doesn't face this dimension of the human condition is incomplete. Somehow, the human mind yearns to know why the innocent suffer without apparent reason, why so many senseless tragedies litter the path of human history. This is the other side of transcendence. Here we experience not the elevation sparked by hearing a "trumpet sound from the hid battlements of eternity" but the existential frustration triggered by a monstrous injustice that seems to have no culprit.

And yet, the mere sense of indignation we experience in the face of innocent suffering points to an innate awareness of what is good and right. How could we recognize something as senseless and rage against it unless we also recognize that there is supposed to be a sense behind things, an order that ought to govern life's events? Where does that come from? Does it not indicate some kind of origin and meaning behind all that exists? The very problem of absurd suffering seems to show us that the world itself is not, or was not meant to be, absurd. Otherwise, what is absurd would be normal, and so would no longer appear absurd.

Evil Choices

The dark side of transcendence doesn't stop there, however. Physical evil is one thing, but moral evil is quite another. Much of humanity's suffering flows not from natural forces outside of human control but from conscious choices made by one person that have dire consequences for others.

In the same gallery where we find Hamilton's depiction of Celadon and Amelia, we also find Ary Sheffer's 1838 painting *Marguerite Leaving Church*. Here again we have a painting depicting a scene from literature, this time from Goethe's nineteenth-century play *Faust*.

Faust is in search of transcendence. He has striven mightily to slake his existential hunger through science and the life of the mind, but he remains unsatisfied. He yearns so desperately to experience whatever it is that will quench his thirst that he turns away from merely human effort and looks toward sorcery. This opens the door for the devil, named Mephistopheles in the play, who offers a deal. If Faust is willing to serve the devil in hell after he dies, Mephistopheles will engineer for him a truly transcendent experience here on earth. The deal is sealed with a drop of Faust's own blood.

The play depicts the intersection of good and evil. Faust's desire for fulfillment is good. His decision to pursue that fulfillment by compromising with Mephistopheles, however, is evil. Evil is personified in the play by the action of an evil spirit. But that evil spirit is not all-powerful. Mephistopheles deceives and seduces, but in the end, his destruction is wrought because of Faust's own tragic, sinful decision. This rings true for everyone who reflects on their own human experience. Our spiritual inclinations, our thirst for transcendence, are not automatically fruitful. Not every answer to our existential questions produces good results.

Sheffer's painting depicts the moment in which Faust first sees Marguerite, with whom he falls immediately in love.

She is shown leaving church, prayer book and rosary in hand, dressed in white and shining with the brilliance of her own purity and goodness. To the side, Mephistopheles whispers in Faust's ear as Faust himself gazes at the young woman with a disconcerting, almost maniacal fascination and lust. His deal with Mephistopheles enables him to garner supernatural help to seduce Marguerite, and the drama ensues.

In the play, Faust's desperate collusion with evil ends up leaving a trail of human wreckage in its wake: Marguerite inadvertently kills her own mother; Faust kills her brother; their illicit union produces an illegitimate child; in her shame and despair, Marguerite murders the child and is condemned to death herself.

The painter chose to depict the moment in the story when moral evil first conceives its tragic offspring: the moment when the devil seizes purity and goodness through the twisted yearnings of a brilliant man who was spiritual (in pursuit of transcendence and meaning) but not religious, not humble enough to accept the limitations of his own nature and trust in the divine design. Instead, he impatiently and recklessly grasps for supernatural power, compromising his own humanity and spreading misery to those he loves most.

Perhaps the most disturbing aspect of the painting is the expression on Mephistopheles's face. He grins broadly as he sows his seeds of destruction, delighting in advance at the anguish and torment he knows will flow from his deal with Faust. This is the heart of evil: rejoicing in the suffering of others and egging on decisions that will lead to such unnecessary suffering, the more intense the better, from Mephistopheles's perspective.

How can we understand that? Where do we locate that reality in the landscape of our minds? How can we reconcile our experiences of transcendent goodness and the spiritual satisfaction they give with this other side of our human condition? We yearn for an answer to the question of moral evil as much as we yearn for an answer to the question of physical evil: where do they come from; why do they afflict us? But mere spirituality cannot supply the answer to such inherently religious questions.

Evil Spirits

Yet a third painting hangs in the same gallery as *Marguerite Leaving Church* and *Celadon and Amelia*. Henry Fuseli's 1781 painting *The Nightmare* depicts yet again another beautiful young woman clothed in brilliant white. This woman is sleeping fitfully, as evidenced by her elongated posture and the position of her arms thrown above her head, which is sliding off the side of her bed. She is the midst of a nightmare. The viewer sees what she feels. Looking on from the background, a weird horse's head with bulging eyes and grinning snout peers invasively at the vulnerable figure. A heavy and threatening demonic figure sits on her chest, pinning her down, constricting her breath, and creating a sense of oppression and panic. The incubus, though sitting toward its victim's face, is actually turning its own face out toward the viewer, breaking through the fourth wall of the scene so as to involve the viewer in the violent encounter. The rich colors and stark contrasts of the painting create an attraction and fascination, even while the almost tangible presence of evil stirs up repulsion and fear.

Throughout the history of religion, dreams and nightmares have often served as a realm of encounter between the spiritual and material worlds. Some religious rituals even use drugs to create an altered state in which shamans or other adherents may more easily receive messages or even revelations about their personal identity through the extraordinary internal events stimulated by the substance.

The specific experience depicted by Fuseli is not entirely fantastic. Awaking in the middle of the night and feeling both an evil presence and a physical, oppressive weight on one's chest is an experience often described by people to priests or other spiritual guides. And contrary to what many secular scholars predicted in the early twentieth century, the emergence of the psychological sciences has not eliminated the need for exorcists, though different experts would give different explanations about why that is the case. (An engraved reproduction of this painting actually hung in Sigmund Freud's Vienna apartment in the first part of the twentieth century.)

The spiritual domain has long been understood to contain not only the spiritual realities corresponding to our experience of transcendence but also spiritual beings, not all of which are guaranteed to be friendly. Venturing into the spiritual realm, whether inadvertently as in the case of Fuseli's sleeping woman or purposely as the case of Faust, involves risking an encounter with a malevolent spirit who may somehow induce suffering.

Many who claim to be spiritual but not religious fail to take this into account or to accept the possibility. But then how do we explain our various experiences of evil? How do we explain the other side of our spiritual experiences? Loneliness often feels as real as love. Despair feels as real as hope. Brokenness and woundedness accompany each one of us, directly or indirectly, as surely as our achievements and satisfactions. We, like Faust, sometimes make choices that damage ourselves and those around us, piling real guilt on top of our equally real weakness. In the face of these uncomfortable realities, part of our search for transcendence and meaning involves a search for protection, safety, healing, and forgiveness.

Light in the Darkness

The complexity of human suffering, especially its spiritual and moral dimensions as exhibited by the three paintings we have been considering, indicates the characteristics of a satisfying answer to our questions about it. We must be able to explain not only where evil comes from but also why we ourselves make compromises with evil, how to resist its seductions, how to bear the suffering it causes us, how to recover from our own moral failures, and how, finally, to escape from its influence. These are spiritual questions because they touch on our experience of what makes life worth living. But their answers will always involve some kind of religious affirmation (or denial) because they are questions of origin and destiny. Even in this mysterious realm of suffering and angst, we see that spiritual but not religious is not enough.

In my own journey, I have never found a more satisfying paradigm for the explanation of evil than that offered by the Judeo-Christian tradition, which points to the existence of corrupt spiritual beings (demons) who corrupted the Creator's original design for the human family by inducing our first parents to sin, to rebel against God's wise and loving plan (this is known as original sin). The goodness we find in our experience here on earth is linked to the original goodness of that plan, and the brokenness we encounter flows from that rebellion's consequences as they reverberate down through the centuries.

Only in the Catholic Church did I find a satisfying path out of that brokenness. The Catholic sacraments, especially the sacrament of confession, affirm both sides of transcendence: the spiritual nobility of our true selves and the spiritual corruption of our fallen nature. Human life from the Catholic perspective is a journey never exempt from struggle and battle against evil forces; that was Jesus's experience, and it is the universal experience of human beings in this fallen world. But in the Church, that journey includes the entirety of our human nature by offering spiritual healing and strengthening through material encounters (sacraments like Baptism, confession, and Holy Communion). The grace of those sacraments, as evidenced over and over again in the lives of saints in every generation, also assures tangible progress in spreading goodness and rolling back the powers of darkness. The Catholic worldview enables us to live peacefully amid the contradictions of a broken world, avoiding both the deathtrap of despair and the seduction of cynicism. Evil is real, but it is not all-powerful, and it doesn't have the last word.

9

Spirituality and Truth:
The Search for Enlightenment

A healthy community is one of our spiritual longings, as are our desires for justice, forgiveness, and healing. But we have other spiritual longings as well. The longing for truth is one often overlooked in today's supposedly post-truth culture. But the search for meaning in this material world cannot simply dismiss something that has occupied some of humanity's greatest creative efforts over the course of more than five thousand years. We need to stop and explore this yearning if we want to do justice to the *spiritual but not religious* paradox.

Oh Happy Truth!

One of my earliest memories is when I first learned to read. I hadn't even begun to go to school yet when my mother took me along to the Bainbridge library in the suburbs of Cleveland, where I grew up. She plopped me down at a kids' table and gave me a Dr. Seuss book.

I still remember opening the book and becoming engrossed in it. I don't remember what my mom was doing.

She may have been reading along with me, or maybe she was occupied with something else. I am not sure. I just remember turning the pages and seeing illustrations going along with a play on the words "whole" and "hole." I looked at the illustrations, and the words, turned the pages, looked again. Then the light bulb went on. Somehow my mind made the connection. I recognized the relationship between the picture of a hole and the word "hole." I recognized the relationship between the picture of a whole pie (contrasted with a pie missing some slices) and the word "whole." I understood that the words *meant* what the pictures *showed*. I had learned the meaning of those words.

The experience was no matter-of-fact development. It sparked intense emotion. Excitement and elation bubbled up within me, filled me, and even overflowed as I shared my discovery with my mom. In fact, I think this is one of my earliest memories. I felt *so happy* having learned the truth about those words and what they meant. It wasn't a happiness linked to anything except the discovery itself. I didn't know, at least at first, that entirely new worlds were opening up to me now that I could read. I couldn't anticipate the later joys that would come from meeting the characters in stories and sharing their adventures. It wasn't that kind of happiness. It was the sheer delight of finding and assimilating a new bit of *truth*. The sheer delight of being enriched in my mind by new knowledge. The meaning of those words was true, and discovering it led me to learn that truth and acquiring that knowledge gave me deep satisfaction. It was similar to the satisfaction that comes from eating when we are hungry or drinking when we are thirsty. But the intensity of the delight was much greater, and it seemed to inhabit a different, deeper place in my mind. Looking back on it now, I believe it was one of my earliest spiritual experiences; that taste of truth was my first taste of transcendence.

Every human person who has the good fortune to develop normally experiences this kind of satisfaction. We learn things. We discover that *this is the way things are,* and it fills our souls with a simple joy, the joy of new knowledge. Somehow, just as our bodies are made in such a way that they can ingest and derive physical nourishment and refreshment from food and drink, our minds are made in such a way that they can ingest truth and derive spiritual nourishment and pleasure from doing so.

Truth's Sad Relatives

The recent advance of relativism in popular culture has clouded our awareness of this capacity built into our nature. Relativism claims that there is no absolute, no lasting and dependable, truth; all truth is relative to some other truth, which means that truth is always changing. Something we know as true today may not be true tomorrow. Relativism emerged partially from the experience of scientific advancement (which has involved a constant evolution of theories about the material universe) and partially from the moral crisis of Western civilization (which reflected a kind of despair at the apparent variety of moral standards found in different human groups), though in its essence, it has always been with us. The cynics of ancient Greece were early relativists, and Buddha's Four Noble Truths are deftly limited to

existential affirmations without offering a definitive onto-
logical system. Relativism is not so new a phenomenon as
some of its critics claim.

I ran into relativism when I went to college. I can still
remember late-night conversations with very thoughtful fellow students in which we had to deconstruct our very language in order to grapple with the possibility that there was
no truth. One conversation about the nature of happiness
lasted for a few weeks. We actually had to stop using the
word happiness to make progress in our conversation about
it. We substituted a technical term, "palm-tree." Does palm-
tree [happiness] exist? If so, is it the same for each person?
How could it be when different people like so many different things?

I understood the appeal of relativism. If truth were relative, then personal preferences would be all-powerful, which
would mean that *I* am all-powerful. If we do not have to
adjust our minds to *the way things are*, our minds can be
free to create a customized, and therefore intensely personalized and intensely comfortable, reality. If we do not have
to adjust our behaviors to an objective moral standard, to
the way one ought to behave, then we can freely give in to the
whims and pleasures of the moment. Something is attrac-
tive, even enticing, about that view of things. It is a heady
and seductive doctrine that claims the human person is powerful enough to autonomously create the very objects of our
deepest needs. If that is the case, the human being becomes
godlike. We become the source of the transcendence we
yearn for. If that happens, we have no need of anything or
anyone else. Absolute self-sufficiency, at least theoretically,

offers liberation from frustration, pain, and all the suffering that comes from the experience of unfulfilled desire.

Yet, in the darkness of that solipsism, we lose the joy of enlightenment. If no truth exists to discover, the joy of discovery disappears. That is what has happened, to a large extent, in a popular culture infected with relativism.

The underdevelopment of the mind's ability to think, and therefore discover new truths, is also encouraged by the tsunami of sensory stimulation so characteristic of the digital age. Certainly, digital technology can be used to stimulate learning (though any efforts to do so operate on the assumption that truth can be known—flying in the face of relativism). But the general environment of popular culture appeals more habitually and vociferously to stimulating the senses, and through them the emotions. Logical thought and patient reasoning are not the natural product of a digital environment in which the average American is bombarded with upwards of ten thousand brand messages each day and switches screens twenty-one times per hour. A culture where some experts estimate the average attention span has diminished to eight seconds is less likely to encourage experiences of authentic intellectual discovery and more likely to habituate us to experiences of immediate sensory and emotional gratification.

Such an environment also squeezes out the time and space needed to *enjoy* truth when we do discover it. An event like learning the difference between "hole" and "whole" will have much less space to resonate and spark delight when the medium used to facilitate it is flashing and warbling and frantically moving on, as the digital world tends to do.

Add to these external challenges—relativism and the digitalization of our social milieu—an internal challenge and we get a fuller portrait of what this search for enlightenment really entails.

The Hard Truth

It takes effort to think. Studying requires hard work. We make mistakes along the way. We run across contradictory opinions and have to deal with them. We get stuck and can't figure things out. Not every assignment and discussion brings about the joy of a four-year-old discovering what "hole" means.

Somehow, truth isn't always easy to find. Not all conundrums are resolved by paging through a Dr. Seuss book. As we have seen, many intelligent people through the millennia have proposed as true starkly different answers to very important questions. Not all these different answers can be equally accurate—some things just don't fit into the description of an elephant.

This in itself requires explanation. If our minds are somehow wired to find and delight in truth, why do disagreements pop up at every juncture of the quest for understanding? Why do some persevere in the search and others throw in the towel? One of the truths of the human condition is that our human nature has to labor mightily to discover the truth, and sometimes even then it falls short.

Nevertheless, we all have experienced the joy of enlightenment. We have been enriched by learning something, by discovering a truth outside of ourselves.

This simple reality made it impossible for me to accept the relativist dogma during my university years. Relativists may be able to convince themselves that they are the one truth and the world is infinitely malleable, but if that's the case, how do we explain learning to read? Or learning to play chess? Or learning to cook? Or, for that matter, learning the latest gossip? How do we explain the experience of discovering and acquiring knowledge and the satisfaction it gives?

As a little boy in the library, I *discovered* the meaning of the words "hole" and "whole." I didn't invent them. I invented plenty of things when playing in the sandbox or in the woods. And inventing things was certainly fun in its own way. But the experience of discovering a truth that was out there, that existed prior to and outside myself, learning it, acquiring knowledge of it, was a different kind of experience entirely. That is an experience of spiritual discovery that brings spiritual delight. If relativism (the doctrine that there is no truth) is actually true (a self-contradiction that doesn't seem to bother the relativists), such experience is not real. (But how can I deny its reality when I felt it so deeply?) If such experience *is* real, then relativism *can't* be true.

Coming to know a truth, any truth, shows that our minds are capable of knowing things, just as one bite of an apple shows that our bodies are capable of eating things. Knowing the truth, learning *how things are,* is part of our human experience. The search to discover and delight in what is true is part of our spiritual DNA. Denying it entails starving an essential part of our humanity. Accepting it and freely engaging in it entails taking steps down the path of wisdom.

Wisdom and Reality

Who doesn't want to be wise? A computer isn't wise. Wisdom is more than just the accumulation of knowledge. Wise people have learned to taste and savor what is true to the extent that they can safely guide others through uncertainty and darkness. The wise have a certain quality about them. Their presence is redolent with their wisdom such that even being with them brings delight and vitality. They are filled with spiritual light, and they bring their light to others. To interact with someone who is wise stirs up our desire to share in that wisdom. It is the best tonic to jar us out of the numbing dead end of cynicism and relativism.

If something is real, it is true. The questions we ask of reality as we strive to understand it reveal rich and complex depths within what is real. That we have not yet been able to exhaust these depths should stimulate us to continue exploring, not lead us to question the very capacity to encounter reality and find truth. In a sense, this inexhaustible complexity, which attracts the mind's attention and invites the mind's exploration, is itself a door to transcendence. If tasting a bit of truth yields as much satisfaction as it does, we can't help but wonder about the source of that truth, about what makes true things true, about what makes real things real. Here again we see that being open to spiritual experience, unlike the closed system of relativism, directs us beyond that experience to questions of origin and meaning, to religious questions.

If what is real is true, then the wise are those who are in greater harmony with reality itself because they have had more thoughtful experiences of reality and thus come to greater, deeper, and more resonant knowledge of what is true. This wisdom enables them not only to perceive reality more fully but to make better choices about how to live in sync with reality.

In that sense, wisdom is more than just knowledge. Many knowledgeable people are not wise. Maybe that's because they haven't been allowed—or they haven't allowed themselves—to delight in the truths they have come to know. When knowledge is just an instrument for ambition, for example, it can lose its savor. But unless we take the time and exercise the humility to savor the truths we learn, just simply as truths, as realities, how can they enrich us? Here the obstacle to enlightenment isn't the ideology of relativism or the deafening cacophony of the digital continent but the frenetic pace of life that inhibits us from being fully present in each moment of our experience. That's what is traditionally called the rat race. But it has become the new normal in our globalized culture.

Maybe we are meant to live in communion with truth, not just use truth to out climb our neighbor up the ladder of success. Perhaps children feeling wonder as they discover themselves and the world around them are more deeply spiritual than the scientist who has inadvertently traded away the capacity for awe in pursuit of awards. Perhaps opening ourselves up once again to discovering and experiencing, deeply and personally, that *this is the way things are* will lead our spiritual journey out of its self-referential spiral and into a path of growing satisfaction. There is one way to find out.

A Curious Claim

In my own spiritual journey, running across the Catholic Church's point of view regarding truth was a mighty challenge. Catholic tradition has what is called the "Magisterium," which is described as the God-given and God-guaranteed capacity to teach truth when it comes to points of religious faith and moral goodness. Throughout its two-thousand-year history, the Catholic Church has continued to teach certain truths about God, the world, and human beings in spite of direct persecution and immense cultural transformations. Empires have come and gone, philosophies have blossomed and faded, but the Catholic Catechism today teaches the same truths that Catholics believed in the time of Christ, even if the way of expressing those truths has altered in different epochs and cultural contexts. The implications of the truths have been emphasized and interpreted differently depending on changing historical circumstances. But "thou shalt not commit adultery" and "Jesus rose again from the dead on the third day" (and similar affirmations) have been held, taught, passed on, and celebrated non-stop in the Catholic world for more than two millennia. As I studied the history, that simple fact became all the more impressive because I saw that the men and women who made up the Church were consistently fallible and undependable. Yet their fallibility and undependability didn't corrupt the deposit of teaching that made up the core of the Catholic faith. How could that be?

When I first encountered the Catholic Church, I was coming from a Protestant background. And as a good Protestant,

I was convinced that the final word on contested issues of religious and moral truth lay with me; that is, with my personal (though, I hoped, Holy Spirit inspired) interpretation of the Sacred Scriptures. Gradually, in light of Catholic claims to an objectively authoritative interpretation of those same Scriptures, I began to wonder about that. Maybe the realm of religion—where the deepest questions were answered—was more like Dr. Seuss than I had previously imagined. Maybe religious truth was *out there* to be discovered, as I had discovered the truth about the words "hole" and "whole." Maybe I didn't have to invent or decide for myself what the universe was like; maybe I could experience the joy and delight and fulfillment of simply discovering it.

If the search for enlightenment truly is part of our spiritual DNA, as we all experience it to be, then we can all look forward to finding eternal light and adjusting our lives to what it shows us rather than pretending to author it ourselves.

10

Spirituality and Goodness: The Search for a Job Well Done

Truth isn't the only thing we long for. Enlightenment always translates into action. Right action, right doing—this, too, is something we yearn for. No human person is completely passive. We are compelled from within to do things, to make things, to decide things. This, too, is connected to our experience of and search for transcendence, if only we take the time to reflect on it. And that's what this chapter will try to address.

Good vs. Bad

We often say, or hear others say, "He is a good person," or something to that effect. We generally know what that means. A certain goodness dwells within a good person, and that person can be counted on to express the goodness within by making good choices, by doing good deeds. When we describe someone as a *bad* person, we are commenting on a quality we perceive that makes someone not good. A certain badness inhabits a bad person, who then exudes this badness in destructive behaviors and choices.

That's the basic distinction. Goodness is constructive, and badness is destructive. A good person tends to help other people flourish, whether in simple ways, like giving them a hand with their groceries, or in deeper ways, like comforting them in times of sorrow. A bad person, on the other hand, isn't interested in helping other people flourish. Bad people are either indifferent to what will help others or they use others to pursue their own ends or they somehow derive a twisted pleasure from making others suffer, from destructive behaviors.

Behind these epithets of good and bad, we find, once again, a presupposition about what it means to be human. Even though a bad person may derive pleasure or a subjective sense of fulfillment from abusing other people, we instinctually recognize something wrong in that. They may think they are flourishing through engaging in that behavior, but if their flourishing leads systematically to others being severely *impeded* from flourishing, something is wrong. Earlier, we examined this presupposition in the context of our search for community. Now we will examine it in a more individual sense, in light of our search for the satisfaction that comes from doing good, from a job well done.

And that is a feeling of satisfaction that we can all relate to. Somehow, when we do something well, when we achieve something, it brings us satisfaction. Just as discovering a new truth brings the delight of discovery, regardless of the usefulness of that newly discovered truth, so too doing a good job, or performing a good deed, brings the satisfaction of a job well done, regardless of the reward or recognition that may (or may not) come with it.

The distinction between performing a good deed and doing a good job is worth pausing on. Doing a good job means achieving a particular goal or result. To achieve that goal requires determination, effort, perseverance, and sometimes other qualities like creativity and the employment of particular skills. When we set ourselves a goal and we strive to achieve it, we set out on a path not only of production but of personal enrichment. By investing our energy and effort—mental, physical, and emotional—in a task, we somehow invest our very selves in it. When it comes out well, we experience a sense of fulfillment. Exercising our capacity to do things, to make a positive difference in this world (even a small difference), feels right.

As human beings, we possess the potential to act, to impact the world around us. Activating this potential by achieving something constructive gives us the interior delight of accomplishment. This delight precedes any recognition by others. We can see that clearly by reflecting on the experience of children. When children work hard on a little art project, pouring themselves into their creative endeavor, they finish it with a real sense of accomplishment and delight. That sense of accomplishment is prior to the pleasure they get from having someone important in their lives recognize it. In fact, their eagerness to show their painting to mom or dad flows from the very delight they have already experienced by finishing their project. Precisely because they have done a good job, and they recognize that by the sense of accomplishment they experience, they want to share it with people they care about. If they didn't experience the prior satisfaction of a job well done, they wouldn't feel eager to share it with others.

The experience of satisfaction coming from a job well done is a clue about who we are as human beings and where we will find the transcendent fulfillment we long for. We are meant to make a difference. When we invest in improving the world around us, we are being true to ourselves.

But there are many different kinds of achievements. Some are more lasting than others. Cutting the grass brings a certain amount of satisfaction, but planting and cultivating a beautiful garden over the course of years, and knowing that the garden will be a place of relaxation and joy for many people, brings a different amount and quality of satisfaction. It seems that the bigger and longer-lasting the impact of our achievements, the greater the satisfaction that will come from them. This is why we find ourselves thirsting for recognition and rewards. When the people acknowledge the value of our work, we receive a validation, an assurance that the effort we poured into this or that task or achievement was worthwhile. In any case, the satisfaction that we experience is spiritual; it corresponds to a sense of inner enrichment that transcends the material benefits.

The Recognition Trap

Sometimes, the recognition we hope to receive from others becomes the very goal we seek. This turns something positive into something negative. Positively, desiring recognition from our fellow human beings for our good achievements shows our connectedness to others. We really are meant to live our lives with others and to put our own energy, creativity, and effort at the service of some kind of work that will benefit the whole community. Although the primary sense of accomplishment we experience when we make a positive impact comes simply from the fruitful investment of ourselves and our potential in the world, the very fruitfulness of that investment is related to our social nature. If our achievements benefit only ourselves, they are poor achievements. The natural desire for recognition reflects this noble instinct of the human spirit, this inclination to make a positive impact on the world around us and therefore on the lives of others.

Too often, however, this thirst for recognition becomes disordered. When the recognition itself is the goal, we lose sight of the good rendered by the constructive achievement. In other words, we are no longer seeking primarily to engage our potential in contributing something good to the world. Rather, we are seeking to elevate ourselves. *We* become the goal. This is a form of selfishness, and it brings us back to our description of a bad person. A bad person focuses so much on self that other people become tools, which can be ignored or used and then thrown away. The distortion inherent in such an attitude is more obvious in dramatic cases like sociopathic abusers or murderers. But the same dynamic is at work in any solely or primarily self-referential exertion of human potential. And working not for the good of a constructive achievement but for the recognition that comes from it is self-referential.

In a self-referential dynamic, we open the door to using destructive means to achieve an apparently good end. If I want to win an Academy Award just for the sake of being recognized, I may engage in corruption or manipulation or even extortion to gain the votes I need. If I want to become a senator just for the sake of being recognized and adored, I can easily give in to the temptation to cheat, flatter, or make unfair, under-the-table deals to influence the election results. When we are focused on the good itself—creating a beautiful work of art in the first case, or protecting and promoting the common good in the second case—we will be much less likely to make destructive choices along the way. And then the recognition we do receive will be all the more satisfying because we will know that we truly did make a positive impact; our achievement is not just a memorable headline but the memorable headline reflects the value of something good that was achieved.

The recognition trap affects us more than we realize. In a consumer society where so many products are available on a market that really does reflect the relationship between supply and demand, fashions impact value and image impacts actions. If one family in the neighborhood invests in a luxury car, other families may feel a subtle (or not so subtle) pressure to measure up to that standard. The luxury car in this scenario may only be a status symbol, not an intrinsic value for the family who buys it. When we lose sight of the true source of fulfillment that comes from material things—the personal investment that goes into producing them and their actual utility for improving our lives in meaningful ways—we can begin placing excessive importance on appearances, falling into the recognition trap.

Output and Input

When recognition reflects reality, then it enhances our inherently satisfying experience of having done a good job, having activated our personal potential to make a good contribution to the world. But the contribution itself is the authentic source of fulfillment. Even here, however, we need to reflect a little more deeply. The impact our contribution makes on others influences the level of satisfaction, but not so directly as we might think. The output of our activity is not the only factor determining the level of satisfaction it gives us. The input is equally important.

Have you ever noticed that some of the most impressive items on your résumé are not the achievements you most value? Often, the most meaningful things derive their meaning not just from what came out of them but from what we put into them. Often the exercise of natural abilities or skills acquired with natural abilities can produce apparently impressive achievements, but not flow from the heart, from the core of who we are. Mark Twain's most famous and widely read works, *The Adventures of Tom Sawyer* and *The Adventures of Huckleberry Finn,* were not his personal favorites. The book that meant the most to him was a less renowned work written much later in his life, a historical novel called *Personal Recollections of Joan of Arc.* This latter work engaged him for twelve years of research, rumination, and writing—longer by far than any of his other works. And this was the one that meant the most to him. Somehow, he had poured more of himself into the process, even though the final product didn't achieve the same literary heights as his other works. It was the input—his own experience of pouring himself into his work—that made the difference in his sense of accomplishment, in the meaning of his achievement.

We see the same dynamic at work from the other side of the equation. When someone does something for us, the meaningfulness of it doesn't always reflect the objective excellence of the gift. How often parents have experienced a greater delight in the clumsy, homemade gift full of the sincere, spontaneous, and unhindered love of a child than a pricey present given out of propriety or politeness. Here again, the more intensely personal and heartfelt quality of input has a profound but intangible effect on the spiritual meaning of the material reality. When more love is put into something, more of oneself is put into it, and so that something becomes more valuable, more meaningful, at least to the people directly involved.

In the end, however, this blossoming of the human spirit through making positive impacts on the world, as well as the authentic satisfaction that flows from it, open up a new conundrum. The meaning of our achievements depends on at least two factors: how much of ourselves we put into them and how much of a positive difference they actually make in the world and in the lives of others. The deeper the impact, the more positive the difference. The more lasting the impact, the more positive the difference. But what really lasts? When we pour ourselves—body, mind, and spirit—into some great enterprise, aren't we pouring ourselves into something destined to disappear? And isn't that a waste of oneself?

If you have ever wandered through the ruins of an ancient city, you can understand the pathos of this question. All things in this world pass away. Rubbing one's hand along the fallen marble columns of an ancient temple, we feel amazed to be in contact with something so venerable, but we also feel the sadness of knowing that all which its builders worked and fought for has crumbled into pieces, and will continue to crumble until nothing remains. Only one of the Seven Wonders of the Ancient World is still with us (the Pyramids of Giza). This material world is inherently tempo-rary. This is the context where action and meaning collide, where our spiritual search for a job well done opens up into the realm of transcendence. What does it really matter if we contribute a little bit to the society in which we live for seventy or eighty years if we are soon to be no more and if the society itself may disappear or morph into something entirely different in a few centuries or millennia?

The Reward From Doing Good

There are two possible avenues we can follow to answer this question. The first brings us back to where we started. The sense of accomplishment we get from a job well done doesn't come just from doing the job. Somehow, doing the job sat-isfies a need we find deep within our souls, a need to give of ourselves for the good of others, a need to put our energy and creativity to work in the world in a constructive way. When we do so, we do something good that doesn't just come from the product; it comes from having done something worth-while, something useful. Regardless of the actual impact on others, we already experience a sense of fulfillment simply from having done something good. We feel that we have been enriched, we are better, more complete, because of the work we have done.

This sheds light on that other side of goodness, the kind we refer to when we say someone is a good person. Someone can *produce* extremely good things without *being* particularly good. The useful good isn't the only good. There is also the moral good, the quality of goodness dwelling within a person whose habitual disposition is to be constructive, not destructive, self-giving instead of self-referential. This quality is independent of the result of the job that was well done. It inheres in the person. If I spend time and energy lovingly cleaning the windows and an hour later a rain storm dirties them again, I still remain enriched by having done something good, something constructive.

This enrichment flowing from doing *something* good also flows simply from *doing good*, from doing what is right—what is in itself constructive and not destructive. This is why simple acts of virtue are their own reward. When we lie, we don't experience the sense of internal gratification that comes from telling the truth. When we lose our patience, we later regret it, even wishing we could go back and replay the interaction so as to stay calmer and more respectful. When we neglect a loved one in need, we may distract ourselves with the pleasure we get from following our momentary whims, but that pleasure leaves us with a sense of emptiness, not the fullness that comes from doing good.

Certain types of behaviors are good for the human spirit, and these are traditionally called virtues. That word comes from a Latin term etymologically linked to words meaning "human" and "strength." Certain types of behaviors—good behaviors—actually enrich us, they make us more fully human, they nourish the unfolding of our true human identity, they are in harmony with what makes the human heart expand and flourish. Just as sunshine is good for a maple tree, and so its leaves spread out to drink it in, so virtuous behavior is good for the human spirit, and we find ourselves inclined toward doing good just because it is good. When we freely second that inclination by making choices in accordance with it, we somehow grasp that goodness, absorbing it as leaves absorb sunshine, and it strengthens and feeds our spirit.

And so, even though doing a good job may not produce an everlasting material result, if we do that good job in such a way that we are at the same time simply doing good—acting virtuously—the goodness will indeed last. It will last by how it enriches our soul and contributes to making us into good people. When we do a good job for the wrong reasons—as in the cases that fall under the recognition trap—the results of our labors may truly enrich the human community, but we may find ourselves empty because what we put into the good job wasn't truly from our hearts, truly an act of self-giving. Rather, it was contaminated by a self-referential kind of self-seeking—the kind that, when repeated, gradually makes a person bad.

A Conscience Question

Doing good, doing what is right—what authentically helps construct a flourishing human community—is the true source of lasting satisfaction when it comes to the choices we make and the actions we engage in. What is good, in this sense, corresponds to what we discussed earlier about what is true, or real. Just as grasping the truth with our minds produces a correlative delight that reveals how our minds are apt for knowing truth, choosing the good with our will produces an interior satisfaction that reveals how our wills are apt for doing good, for contributing creatively to the world around us. A job truly well done includes not only doing the job well but also doing good while doing the job.

This is where conscience enters the discussion. Usually, we use the term "conscience" to refer to that inner voice telling us which is the right thing, the good thing, to do. That same voice approves us after we choose what is right and good. It also accuses us after we choose what is evil. Unless we follow the lead of our conscience, we simply cannot live with interior peace.

Unfortunately, however, the voice of conscience can sometimes err. A child who grows up among thieves, whose parents and other relatives make their living through crime, may grow up with a malformed conscience, believing that certain behaviors are in themselves good and constructive when in fact they are evil and destructive. To persevere acting according to a malformed conscience requires turning a blind eye to the destruction one's evil deeds cause. That such blindness has appeared so frequently and lasted so stubbornly throughout human history is one of the great mysteries wrapped up in the question of evil we discussed earlier.

Some philosophers and psychologists have tried to solve that mystery by claiming the voice of conscience is a purely social construct. But this is an oversimplification. That the human conscience can be malformed through noxious influences during our formative years is one thing. To conclude from such an undeniable reality that therefore the conscience is a pure social construct without any reference to objective goodness at all is quite another thing.

A Lighthouse in the Fog

The experience of satisfaction that comes from doing good and from doing a good job can serve as our lighthouse amid the fog caused by the mystery of evil. It reveals that human nature is real and that certain actions allow it to flourish, just as certain conditions allow a maple tree to flourish. The difference between the human nature and the maple tree nature is that the human nature includes a spiritual quality of freedom. A maple tree will flourish in the right conditions no matter what; it has no conscious choice in the matter. Human beings, however, will flourish only when they choose to act in accordance with their good, when they choose to do a good job and to do good doing it.

Doing a good job, and the satisfaction it gives, clues us in to our inherent creativity, our interior impulse not only to react the world around us, like squirrels and spiders, but to contribute to that world, to engage our potential, effort, talent, and skill to make a positive impact. The deeper and more lasting satisfaction that comes simply from doing good, from choosing to act virtuously regardless of the useful results, is even deeper. And it clues us in to our spiritual nature, to the deeper meaning behind our presence here in this material world. Somehow, we are meant not just to make the world a better place; we are also meant to make ourselves better, to develop the potential goodness within us. Perhaps that is the greatest contribution any human being can really make to this passing world.

And yet, even that contribution seems to be passing. Not only ancient temples fall to the ground and crumble into dust as the millennia unfold, but every human being does too. We all die sooner or later. Does the goodness inherent in our souls, the goodness accumulated through decades of doing good while tallying up jobs well done, die with us? If so, can we really insist that doing good truly is meaningful?

This is where our discussion of the search for goodness necessarily transitions out of mere spirituality and into religion. Above all, the lasting quality of goodness touches on the religious question of our destiny. Can we hope for life after death? Can we hope that goodness makes a contribution not only to this passing world but also, somehow, to a world that will not pass away?

A War of Worldviews

The questions of origin and destiny separate most starkly the religious and secular worldviews. The secular worldview simply assumes that this world—this *saeculum,* which is the Latin term for this present age, this present world of time and space—is all there is. The idea of a spiritual realm that transcends this world is foreign to the secular mindset. The idea of a spiritual realm—a realm outside the time and space of this material world—inhabited by spiritual beings is equally preposterous. The idea of a divinity that explains the ultimate origin and destiny of all things is simply discarded by secularism.

And yet, the question still arises in the human heart: this goodness that I am moved to pursue, to grasp, to activate, does it really mean anything? If nothing lasts beyond this age, if all things are destined to crumble into dust, then where is the meaning of goodness? And if there is no meaning, why do we find ourselves thirsting for it? How could a desire exist without a corresponding reality that can fulfill it?

The existence of life after death is an almost universal conviction among religions. A secularist may write that off as pre-scientific superstition. But we have to ask ourselves, does modern science really prove the non-existence of life after death? Is that even something that falls within the purview of the scientific method? After all, science deals with material things, measurable things. A spiritual realm is by its very nature immaterial, simply outside the reach of the scientific method. Secularists may choose to deny the possibility of life after death, but they may not—at least not fairly—appeal to science as a rational proof of their choice.

And so, the secular worldview must somehow grapple with the last hundred thousand years of human history, in which a spiritual instinct, so to speak, toward life after death has been ever present. If this instinct were just wishful thinking, where did the wish come from? Squirrels and spiders don't make cemeteries. Dogs and cats give no signs of ever having venerated their ancestors. But humans have always done these things. Our experience of transcendence here in an imminent world seems to have made it clear that this world, this *saeculum,* is *not* all there is. The passing nature of all material things cannot explain the mind's grasping of truth, the will's grasping of goodness, the mystery of evil, the human dignity at the core of the common good. There must be something more. If not, even what seems to exist must actually be just an illusion. If there is no transcendent meaning, then there is no meaning at all.

Surprised in a Cemetery

My first summer job found me working in the town cemetery. I was sixteen years old. I would help cut the grass, trim the trees, set up and clean up for funerals, repair old headstones, and put in new ones. I have fond memories of that job. It was meditative. I got to know the different sections of the graveyard, and I would wonder about the lives of the men and women buried there. And, of course, that line of musing led me to wonder about my own life, about what would make it worth living.

That summer, I first ran across the ancient, ubiquitous epitaph:

> All you who pass me by
> As you are, so once was I
> As I am, so must you be
> Prepare for death and follow me

Such a stark expression of an undeniable truth I had never before considered. As I rode by that tombstone on a lawn-mower, reading those words was like hearing a message, and a challenge, from the person whose corpse had been buried underneath it, and indirectly from the hundreds, maybe thousands of other people buried under the grass I was blithely cutting every day. Each one of them had, at some point, been alive. They had their jobs, relationships, families, hopes and their dreams, sorrows and their joys, and achievements and failures. They had been just as I am.

But now as I pass them by, they are no more. At least, it would seem so. Death has claimed them. Death has put an end to their journey. No one escapes death. The evidence was all around me. But if death is the final note for the symphony that is every life on earth, then what is the meaning of all our struggles and our striving? How does one prepare for death if nothing comes after death? And if this world is all there is, how does one explain the experience of transcendence, the grasping of truths that, unlike marble temples, do not change with the passing of time, the satisfaction and peace that come from a job well done and from doing good?

The question of destiny brings us also back to our search for a happy ending. If the material world is all there is, and if that world ends in death, how can we explain the yearning for a happy ending that makes entertaining stories into a source of inspiration? If death truly is the end, then happy endings are not true, not real. But if they are not true and real, why do they resonate so profoundly in our spirits, which only resonate with things that actually exist?

If, on the other hand, life in this *saeculum* is actually some kind of pilgrimage leading to another, transcendent life, then everything changes. Then the good that we do here, which makes us into good people and helps others live full lives, actually has everlasting repercussions. Then the decisions we make along the way of our earthly journey really do matter. Then our experience of satisfaction at a job well done makes sense; it is another one of those trumpets sounding from the hid battlements of eternity. Then every experience of transcendence suddenly becomes not only a boost of spiritual energy but also a promise of things to come and a reading of true north on a spiritual compass. Then we could carve a different epitaph into our headstone:

> All you who pass me by
> As you are, so once was I
> As I am so must you be
> I wish I could show you what I see!

11

Spirituality and the Environment: The Search for Joy

Through the years, I have guided many groups of people through many different museums. Although I often get mixed reactions from our stops in front of works representing cubism or abstract expressionism, paintings of the style known as romanticism always resonate.

The Genius of Romanticism

The romantic painters worked mostly in Western culture, and mostly in the nineteenth century. In a reaction against what they considered overly intellectualized and controlled art, characteristic of the neo-classical style marking the Enlightenment period, these artists looked to the raw power of nature for their inspiration. Many of them traveled widely looking for unspoiled natural landscapes, which they would contemplate and sketch. In their studios, they would often paint from their sketches and their memory, combining elements from different actual landscapes to create canvases capturing the force of natural beauty even when they didn't represent photographic reproductions of existing vistas.

Romanticism was interested in the breathtaking awe stirred up by nature's grand spectacles. Romantic paintings consistently depict human beings, human activities, and human products as small and fragile, almost insignificant in comparison with the imposing and arresting presence of oceans, mountains, forests, storms, waterfalls, and other natural phenomena. They show the drama of nature from a broad horizon, and they spark in the viewer a sense of what the romantics called "the sublime," that particular elevation of the human spirit that happens when we find ourselves suddenly presented with the wondrous spectacle of natural beauty on a large scale.

We have all felt that at some point. Think about the times you may have watched the sun rise or set over the ocean, or over mountains. Think about the view from a mountaintop on a clear day, or the stirring in the soul as you paddle down a wide river flanked with a combination of magnificent trees and sheer bluffs. At times, the natural world seems to overpower us, effortlessly hushing our souls and washing over us, carrying us far away from the normal hustle and bustle of our noisy, mundane worries and concerns. In the interior calm produced by the sublimity of those encounters with nature, we—such finite and limited creatures as we are—feel momentarily connected to the transcendent, the immense, the immeasurable, the undefinable, maybe even the infinite. The experience comes upon us; we cannot manufacture it, and we cannot control it. We can only welcome it and bask in the light of otherworldly glory that has, for some mysterious reason, revealed itself to us in that moment.

Volcanic Beauty

Take, for example, Frederick Church's masterpiece *Cotopaxi,* a South American landscape painting from 1862. The Ecuadorian volcano *Cotopaxi* dominates one side of the painting as it erupts and pours dense smoke and ash into the sky. On the other side, the rising (or setting, commentators don't agree) sun, a piercing orange and yellow ball seemingly doing battle against the volcanic spew, boldly shines through the darkness tinging the entire landscaping with a vibrant, glowing red tone. The horizon also glows with the bright, luminescent sunlight that flows forward to be reflected by the calm surface of the lake, which in turn overflows in a boiling waterfall that plunges through high cliffs in the painting's foreground. A few tall, courageous trees decorate the left foreground. Some of them lean over the cliff, drinking up the spray from the waterfall and revealing a narrow path and a single traveler with his llama, just specks of color barely visible and easily overlooked amid the grandiose drama of the imposing work, which is seven feet wide and four feet high.

Art historians relate the strangely harmonic blending of a volcano's violence and a sun rise's tranquility to the social upheaval caused by the American Civil War, which was in full swing when Church finished his masterpiece. They surmise that Church was offering a vision of hope to a country savagely divided against itself. The subtle cross formed by the sunlight's reflection on the lake's surface is seen as a religious allusion and evidence of such hope. And the stark difference between this later version of the subject and Church's earlier version, in which the volcano was not erupting and the land-scape blossomed with ample tropical flora, may indeed indi-cate that some of the turbulence of the painting reflected the social distress in which Church himself was immersed. But the painting's impression goes far beyond social commen-tary, as is evidenced by its power to arouse reactions of awe and wonder in generations of viewers throughout the last century and a half.

Beyond Ecology

In the face of primeval forces like volcanoes, waterfalls, and the sun, the viewer—like the traveler depicted so minutely in the left foreground of *Cotopaxi*—feels insignificant. We gaze at a cosmic drama, something far beyond our control, or even our influence. Its awful beauty captures and quiets us. Its terrible power threatens us, but at the same time, it fascinates us. In front of this scene, the ordinary, petty, and somewhat chaotic or at least relentless flow of our little lives is interrupted, and we are brought face to face with gran-deur and a glimpse of transcendence. And it resonates with us. It is as if our souls can breathe again when lifted into the rarefied atmosphere of sublime beauty. We feel more at home, more alive even, in the presence of this magnificence. It reminds us of something that the daily grind too often drowns out. It stirs in us something that too often lays dor-mant deep within us: that thirst for *something more* in life, for a deeper meaning, for something sacred. Like a soldier between battles receiving a letter from his fiancée back home sprinkled with her perfume, the beauty of a painting like this clears our minds and refreshes our hearts, making us pause to delight in being alive right now and to look forward to what is still to come.

Romantic paintings recreate the rare and unforgettable experience of nature's sublime beauty. They speak to us of the real value of the natural world, which goes beyond mere existence and survival. The natural world has always sparked spiritual desires in the human heart. We saw this previously in our discussion of early religion, which translated the awe-inspiring capacity of nature's beauty into the worship of nature: if the sublime power of the natural world has the ability to stir up and satisfy our thirst for transcendence, then it must be connected to the source of that transcendence. Through our worship of the mountain, we can reach the spirit beyond the greatness of the mountain, so early religion's logic went.

For human beings, this spiritual, and even religious, dimension of the natural world has always been the more important dimension. Yes, we need the products of nature for our survival—they provide our food, clothing, shelter, and energy—but why is survival important? For human communities, life has always had a deeper meaning than mere survival, even than mere pleasure. Surviving has always been a necessary precondition for *thriving*. And thriving has always involved a cultivation of our spiritual capacities through religious activity.

This is one reason why so many of humanity's greatest artistic achievements have been linked to religion. Nature's sublime beauty opens up our experience of transcendence; the human mind searches through this experience and seeks its origin and its significance; then human creativity strives to make paintings and sculptures and temples that not only imitate nature's beauty but also weave it together into a multi-media tapestry elucidating its deeper—transcendent—meaning and allowing us a chance to enter into communion with it more regularly and fully instead of having to wait helplessly for our next surprise encounter with a volcano at dawn.

A Climate of Beauty

St. Peter's Basilica in Rome, the largest Christian church in the world, is one of these great architectural achievements. I myself have experienced epiphanies of transcendence countless times there. And over and over again, as I have taken visitors into and through this basilica, I have witnessed their countenance transformed by wonder and awe simply as they enter this climate of beauty and gaze for the first time upon its marvels.

And it really is a *climate* of beauty. All great architecture gives shape, form, and expressive character to the space around us. A building is a climate, an environment, just as much as a field, a forest, or an oasis is. Buildings have practical purposes like shelter and protection, but unlike rabbits with their dens or foxes with their warrens, human beings have always infused their buildings with *more* than practical purposes. The activity proper to the place is human activity, and so it shares in the spiritual dimension of the human heart and mind. And if human *activity* has both a practical and a spiritual dimension, then so should the *place* where it occurs. The choice of building material, the arrangement of the different architectural elements, the decor and the dimensions should contribute to creating an appropriate climate for whatever human activity is meant to take place there.

St. Peter's Basilica is at its core a place of Christian worship. And so it has an altar where the sacrifice of the Mass is offered, a nave where worshippers gather to participate in the sacrifice and to offer their prayers, and a narthex, a transitional space between the outside world where daily life ebbs and flows and the interior sacred space where believers can encounter their God and sanctify their daily life with divine grace. Almost all Christian churches have similar basic elements.

But the grandeur of St. Peter's doesn't come from those elements in themselves. Rather, it comes from the particular way of arranging them, an arrangement linked to the meaning of the actual place where the building was constructed. St. Peter was one of Jesus's closest followers, the leader of the band of twelve Apostles chosen by Jesus to spread the Gospel and to build up a worldwide Church to carry on his saving mission through all time and space. He was martyred for his faith in Rome—the city where he had served as bishop and the first pope—around the year AD 64. His fellow Christians buried him in a pagan graveyard near the place of his execution close to Vatican hill. Believers would come to the grave to offer prayers for St. Peter and to ask St. Peter, whom they believed was with Christ in heaven, to pray for them. Eventually a small chapel was built over the grave site to provide a locus for this devotion. In the fourth century, Emperor Constantine sponsored the construction of a magnificent basilica to take the place of the chapel. By the fifteenth century, that basilica had become structurally compromised. The popes at the time, successors to St. Peter as the central authority of the Catholic Church, decided to raze the ancient basilica and build a new one. They garnered the contributions of Michelangelo, Maderno, Brunelleschi, and other outstanding Renaissance and Baroque artists who over the course of almost two centuries constructed and decorated the current structure, whose high altar is located directly above the St. Peter's original grave.

Universality and Unity

This particular place of Christian worship, therefore, has a unique connection to what is known as the Petrine ministry, the specific ministry exercised by popes to maintain unity among all Catholics throughout the world and throughout the ages. As a place, therefore, it evokes the unique combination of universality (extending through all time and space) and unity (one faith, one baptism, one body of believers) so precious to Catholic Christians. The architecture of the basilica is meant to embody, reflect, and communicate that meaning.

And every element does exactly that. First of all, the building itself and the space it encloses are immense. It is more than two football fields in length, five hundred feet wide, and almost five hundred feet high from the floor to the top of its dome. Entering such a space immediately inspires a sense of awe and grandeur akin to what the Romantic painters were trying to capture by creating a visual contrast between the size of their landscapes and the size of the human figures within them. But since a visitor to the basilica actually steps inside the immensity, the intensity of the feeling evoked is arguably much greater.

That immensity manifests the universality of the Catholic faith, safeguarded by the Petrine ministry. A physical climate embodying a spiritual value and stimulating an experience of sublime beauty that enraptures both the body and the spirit—here is the genius of the human heart brilliantly at work.

The naves are lined with majestic statues of saints from every period of the supra-millennial history of the Catholic Church, flanked by altars with monumental marble sculptures and larger-than-life mosaics, and topped with decorated domes and personified figures of all the Christian virtues. These statues and figures are proportionate in size to the dimensions of the building, making them gigantic and giving them all a majestic presence. They intensify the visitor's sense of entering into something truly immense, truly universal.

In spite of the dizzying number of elements and furnishings within the basilica, the space is clearly unified by the central altar and its nine-story high bronze canopy, the baldachin designed and constructed by Rome's greatest Baroque artist, Gianlorenzo Bernini. The entire building revolves around, flows out from, and points back towards that central place, which is directly beneath the 448 feet high central dome, and directly above St. Peter's first-century tomb. This brilliant design brings an indescribable harmony to the myriad features of the sacred environment: the seemingly infinite variety of realities embraced by its universality is brought together in a stable but dynamic unity. Visitors are not just impressed and awestruck by the terrible immensity of it all. At the same time, they are inspired and encouraged through the sense of welcome provided by the unified vision; they feel invited to become part of this place, to become a saint among the saints in this climate of beauty.

Beauty and Spiritual Freedom

And that is the proper feeling, the proper response. Just as an encounter with truth yields the delight of feeling one's soul expanded by the possession of new knowledge, and a job well done enlarges the soul with the satisfaction of having increased the quotient of goodness both in the world and in oneself, of having become better, so too the experience of beauty yields a sense of spiritual enrichment. Whether encountering sublime beauty directly in nature or through the mediation of a painting like *Cotopaxi* or through entering a sublimated space like St. Peter's Basilica, the encounter changes things. The touch of beauty rejoices the soul in a lasting way. We feel better able to endure the heavy burdens of daily drabness. We feel moved to make of our own lives something beautiful, something sublime. We feel more possibilities, more hope that the meaning we yearn for can be found and grasped. We feel that the whispers of our hearts, which so often seem illusory and impractical, are clues to what really matters and will not lead us astray; the experience of beauty sparks a greater spiritual freedom for following wherever they may lead, in spite of conventional wisdom's warnings.

The interior sweetness produced by an encounter with transcendent beauty can be described by no other word than joy. An epiphany in front of a work of art or a majestic sunset enriches us with the experience of joy, of a pleasure so deep that it transcends all merely physical pleasures. It is a spiritual sweetness we cannot deny. A gladness sparked by the material reality though which we glimpsed the beauty, but rooted in something much more lasting, the transcendent source of that beauty. And so beauty, too, brings us to the brink of eternity, and the joy it gives spurs us on to continue searching for Beauty itself.

Perhaps here in the realm of beauty, even more than in the realms of truth and goodness, we intuit the natural connection between spirituality and religion. The interior joy beauty kindles is extremely personal; it *feels* like the result of personalized gift. It seems perfectly fitted to our personal existence and our personal needs and desires that it defies being reduced to the random influence of impersonal forces. When we encounter the sublime and it touches us, we feel *known* and *affirmed* through the experience. As our spirits soar, we yearn not only to savor the experience but to enter into relationship with its source. Beauty, which moves our whole soul so deeply, is simply too perfectly suited to our human nature to be explained by anything but a personalized, transcendent giver, just as a personalized Christmas gift is so much more meaningful than something given generically and out of mere formal obligation. Our experience of beauty shows, undeniably, that the source of all transcendence, the source of all our sublime experiences, is somehow linked to love, and love is always personal. Being honest in the face of such an experience is yet another invitation to allow our spiritual experiences to lead us toward their natural fulfillment in religious commitment.

12

Spirituality and the Incarnation: God's Search for Us

Throughout these chapters, we have reflected on the different experiences we often refer to as spiritual. We have seen that an authentic spiritual experience, precisely because of the depth of its resonance in the human soul, both satisfies our deeper thirsts, and at the same time invites us to search for more. We want to discover how to live more habitually in the spiritual realm, more fully in tune with the transcendent realities we glimpse through our encounters with community, suffering, truth, goodness, and beauty. How can we do that? Where does this transcendence come from? How can I plug into it? How can live in more perfect communion with it? These, we have seen, are the questions that naturally flow from our spiritual experiences, questions whose answers are intrinsically religious. From that perspective, spirituality naturally dovetails with religion. Any religion that kills the spiritual experience has lost its life and meaning; any spiritual experience that stops without continuing the search is a stultified experience.

What Are We Looking For?

Although we have made reference to religion in general, and even taken a brief tour through the history of religion to show how all religions really are the same (they face the same fundamental, existential questions common to the human experience throughout all of history) but are also really different (they give irreconcilably contrasting answers to some of the questions), we have not taken a stand on which religion provides the best answers to those questions.

Honestly reflecting on our spiritual experience, we can identify the parameters of truth for religion. A religion that answers the fundamental questions deeply must make sense of that experience on all levels. It must satisfactorily identify who is human, who belongs to the human community. It must address the undeniable reality of our intellect's capacity to know things and to experience the delight that only comes from real, true knowledge. It must provide practical guidance for our irrepressible desire to contribute something good to the world, as well as our experience of enrichment when we make constructive instead of destructive moral choices. It must provide definitive insight into the origin of the universe and the source of that transcendence we only experience partially and temporarily in our current condition. It must show us how to live in communion with that source, and how to interact with the inhabitants of the spiritual realm. It must indicate our ultimate destiny and explain the resonance we feel with happy endings. It must foster and nurture the interior joy that springs up within us when beauty opens a window to the transcendent. It must shed light on the mystery of suffering caused by both physical and moral evil, as well as our puzzling and self-contradictory capacity to make evil choices. It must account for our whole humanity: both the temporal, material dimension and the spiritual, transcendent dimension.

Anyone who has had an authentic spiritual experience has also experienced, at least vaguely, the deeper reality that gives rise to all spirituality, and thus has indistinctly tasted the food that satisfies our spiritual yearnings. Every spiritual experience involves both the sublime satisfaction that comes when our souls touch the transcendent and also the existential longing that flows from the passing nature of that touch. Spirituality is both the end of a search for something that transcends the unsatisfying experiences of this limited material world and the initiation of new search for greater and greater communion with what transcends this world.

Receiving the gift of a spiritual experience includes receiving a call to continue a spiritual journey, a search for the solidity of religious answers. The gift of a spiritual experience ups the ante, so to speak, and increases the stakes of our own individual existence. Having glimpsed the promised land where alone the human heart will find its home, we now have a responsibility to undertake the journey that will bring us there. To stop merely at the spiritual experience itself, to think that such an experience can satisfy us if only we can find ways to repeat it, thus turning away from the calling, the invitation embedded within that experience, is to close ourselves off from our true potential. The capacity to have a spiritual experience indicates the presence of a capacity to enter into full communion with the sources of all spiritual values. Turning away from the religious search in order to stay merely in the spiritual stimulation that is its origin involves being untrue to our deepest selves. This is why staying at "spiritual but not religious" is so unacceptable; it cuts short the life of the spirit just when it is beginning to blossom, confining the human soul to a self-referentiality that denies its very essence.

The search for meaning in this material world starts with the surprising gift of a spiritual experience, but it mustn't stop there. We must keep searching for the fullness of that experience, for lasting communion with the very source of all that is transcendent. That is, in the end, the only honest and truly human path to follow.

A Change of Perspective

Till now, we have been reflecting on the spiritual and religious journey from our human point of view: How can we understand our transcendental experiences, and how can we follow where they lead—how can we be both spiritual and religious?

Among the world's many religions, the Judeo-Christian tradition (which in this sense includes Islam—all three claim a common spiritual father in the Old Testament figure of Abraham) adds a unique twist to this journey. It presents us with a divinity who does not wait for human beings to find him, who does not stay aloof in an Olympian hideaway while mankind struts and frets its way through life, intervening only on unpredictable whims and needing to be convinced by human effort to wake from its divine indifference to the human predicament. Rather, it presents us with a single, sovereign divinity who took the initiative to create the world out of love, to create the human family to freely join him in developing the potential of this world by being co-creators of human culture. The human family rebelled against this divine plan, under the evil influence of rebel spirits. This broke the harmony of the divinity's original plan and led to the spread of evil, both moral and physical, with its consequences of human suffering.

The divinity responded to this rebellion not with wrath, nor by abandoning his creatures, nor by crumpling up the first creation and starting over. The divine response was, rather, one of mercy in which the source of all things continued to take the initiative, this time by gradually unfolding a plan of redemption in which fallen humanity could regain its communion with the divine—and so find once again the meaning it had forfeited by rebelling against and cutting itself off from God, the meaning which is the only source of true fulfillment for the human heart created to live in that communion—through repentance and faith.

Redemption began with a series of covenants, deeply intimate and interpersonal agreements between the divinity and representatives of the fallen human family. With Abraham, the covenant was linked to a particular people whose identity took shape and developed gradually, through the influence of chosen figures like Moses, David, and the Old Testament Prophets.

This vision of the transcendent realm shared by Judaism, Christianity, and Islam answers the questions of our search for meaning by revealing a God who takes up a search of his own. From creation through redemption, this divinity reaches out toward the human family, searching for our humble, grateful, wise, and loving response to the gifts of existence, life, and spiritual awareness. A God who goes in search of people, not for vengeance or self-aggrandizement, but for their temporal and eternal good is different than those gods who populated primitive and archaic religions. In this vision of divinity, our search for communion with transcendence is met and welcomed by a transcendent, personal God's search for us.

Up to this point, in the unfolding of the Old Testament covenants, the three monotheistic religions of this tradition are in agreement. The understanding of the temporal and transcendent realms, the conception of a divinity who is not only the origin and destiny of the world and human life but who also cares and intervenes benevolently in our lives, and the idea of a human nature intrinsically dignified with a spiritual dimension that can find its fulfillment only through living in communion with the one, true God who is personal, omnipotent, omniscient, and all good are the shared elements in the Judeo-Christian religious tradition. These elements provide unique, intriguing answers to some of the religious questions springing from our spiritual experiences. But the coming of Jesus Christ initiated a divergence of answers to other of those questions, not so much the questions of origin and destiny, but the question of how to enter into and develop life in communion with the Creator and Redeemer of the human family.

Three Divergent Traditions

Christians affirm that the series of Old Testament covenants reached their promised and prophesied fulfillment when the one, true God himself decided to continue his search for us by becoming one of us, by being born as Jesus Christ of the Blessed Virgin Mary. Through the incarnation of God, the transcendent being—the origin of the transcendence at work in all of our spiritual experiences—actually entered into this immanent world. Here, God's search for us took an entirely new turn in the history of religion. By becoming human, God chose to reveal himself to us in a way that would also reveal us to ourselves. Transcendence becomes visible in Christ so that his life and teachings become a place and a vehicle for our full communion with God.

Christ's own famous saying, "I am the way, and the truth, and the life" (Jn 14:6), is a direct answer to the human heart's search for the source of all that is good, true, and beautiful. His revelation that God, the origin of all things, is three persons in one divine nature (the doctrine of the Blessed Trinity) resolves the tension underlying our search for authentic community that integrates each person's individuality instead of enslaving it. His revelation of God's limitless love opens the door to recovery from moral failure (forgiveness of our guilt) through a personal encounter with God's own mercy. And his establishment of a divinely guided and supported spiritual family that extends to every corner of time and space (the Church) delineates a path of prayer, ritual, and behavior that initiates, nourishes, and protects every person's spiritual and religious journey to everlasting communion with God.

The Jewish tradition rejected the Incarnation and the subsequent variations of religious answers offered by Christianity. The Jewish path to communion with God continues to invoke the revelations about God and mankind present in the Old Testament, but it is a path of hope in a Messiah yet to come, not in a Savior now present whose grace is already infusing this world with the spiritual leaven of true, everlasting communion between God and human beings, between the temporal and the transcendent.

The Muslim tradition also rejected the Incarnation, reinterpreting the figure of Jesus as a prophet who had been misunderstood by the Christians. In the figure of Mohammad, who received yet another revelation through an encounter with an angel (the product of which was the Koran), Muslims find the final prophet who corrected the misinterpretations of the Christians and completed the Jewish revelation. Islam's view of the human person and the divinity, like the Jewish view, exclude the many new elements offered through the Christian dogma of the Incarnation. As a result, the path leading to communion with the transcendent God looks very different for a Muslim than for a Christian or a Jew. It consists primarily of pious actions known as the five pillars of Islam: belief in God, ritual prayer, pilgrimage, almsgiving, and fasting.

We find variations within these three monotheistic traditions—different ecclesial communities and denominations in Christianity (Orthodox, Catholic, Anglican, Evangelical, etc.), different branches of Judaism (orthodox, reformed, conservative, etc.), and different schools in Islam (Sunni, Shia, and their sub-groups). Differences of doctrine and practice within each tradition can be sharp, but those differences fall within a shared religious vision clearly distinct from other religions as regards many of the fundamental religious questions.

Nevertheless, whether adherents believe God's search for us will culminate in a Messiah yet to come, has culminated already in a prophetic doctrine, or has gone to the wild extreme of the Incarnation, these traditions stand out among the world's religions precisely because they articulate not only the human search for meaning but a complementary, divine effort to help our search succeed.

Jump-starting the Search

The immediate goal of this extended reflection on what it means to be spiritual but not religious has never been the reader's conversion to a particular creed. Rather, it was a sincere attempt to convince non-religious readers who have had authentic spiritual experiences that those experiences cannot bear lasting fruit on their own. The indescribable satisfaction of an authentic encounter with the transcendent, under any form, is only an appetizer. It promises a fuller satisfaction to come, when we honestly pursue answers to the questions stirred up by that experience. We must not suppress our hunger for meaning, because that hunger, in the end, is connected to the core of what makes us human, the core of our identity. Aborting the search it invites us toward will only rupture our souls and leave us incomplete. If we are spiritual, we owe it to ourselves to continue searching until we become religious, or until we die in the midst of that sincere search.

The treatments in this chapter of the Judeo-Christian religious tradition, along with the treatments in earlier chapters of the different kinds of religions that have marked human history, are meant to help readers overcome any subconscious or emotional prejudice against religion in general. Authentic religion always dovetails with authentic spirituality. Unspiritual experiences of religion happen, and when dramatic, they can create the impression that all religion is actually anti-spiritual. Such an impression can easily stifle a healthy search for meaning, which ultimately leads to an unfulfilled life and to spiritual frustration.

Many readers who consider themselves spiritual but not religious may have traveled just such a path. Their negative, unspiritual experience of religion may have turned them away from even a vague hope that spiritual experiences can truly lead to lasting, religious communion with the divine. And so they have contented themselves with the appetizers.

If these reflections have sparked a curiosity in readers like those, perhaps a good next step would be to go back to their original religious tradition and give it a second chance. Having delved more deeply into the nature of our spiritual experiences and their essential connection to religious questions, perhaps those readers will be better equipped for the search for lasting meaning in this passing, material world. That, at least, is the author's sincere and fondest hope.

A Return to the Museum

In the case of the author himself, my own case, the search for meaning in this material world has been the engine of my life. But in all honestly, and in spite of what many readers may surmise due to my being a Catholic priest, I want to finish by explaining how this search continues, how I haven't stopped searching even though I have found so many answers.

I have come to believe, after much study, exploration, and interaction with adherents of many different religions, that the most satisfying answers to our deepest questions are found in the Catholic faith, the original and the most complete Christian Church. No creed validates and affirms the whole human experience as magnificently as the Catholic creed. And no creed provides such respectful, nuanced, and yet simple and resonant responses to our natural spiritual inquiries about the origin and destiny of all things, and about the path to lasting meaning (the books listed in the appendix offer some excellent explanations of why that is the case).

And yet, my own experience has shown me that even when a true and satisfying answer is found, the human spirit continues wanting more. And this makes sense. We are both material and spiritual. We are finite, but we find a spark of the infinite in our hearts. And so encountering God as he truly is, as he has revealed himself to be through the incarnation of Jesus Christ, is more than simply finding an answer; it is finding a person, a unique person who can really be known, but who at the same time is always able to be discovered anew. Finding Christ and his Church is more than finding a buried treasure; it is finding a relationship (a whole network of relationships, really, when you consider the trans-generational family of believers that comprises the

Church) and a path to be traveled together, a path continually familiar and surprising, old and new, comfortable and jarring. For me, moving along this path has steadily deepened the convictions that anchor me in truth, goodness, and beauty, which in turn has given my life a stability and purpose producing interior peace and joy. I would be remiss if I didn't admit and share that reality. But at the same time, the journey has never ceased to present unforeseen twists and turns, some painful and some delightful. It truly is a journey. It truly is an adventure. Knowing that I am on the right path gives satisfaction, while knowing that more of the path still remains to be explored and discovered as I make my way to my destination gives me a sense of hope and purpose.

The experience of having found answers to my spiritual questions while still continuing to discover all the implications of those answers brings me back to where we started: the Gallery of the Muses.

The great museums of the world have many, many floors, and each floor has many wings, and each wing has many rooms, and each room has many works of art, and each individual work of art opens a window into myriad layers of human experience and endless vistas of transcendence. Just so, as I have come to embrace and attempt to live out the Catholic faith, every step of the way I have found myself led through doors and passageways always opening onto new wings, with an abundance of new rooms, with an endless collection of new spiritual and religious vistas. Taking the humbling but liberating step of committing myself to the religious truth of Catholicism, far from cutting me off from the richness of spiritual experience, has enhanced that experience, over and over again. Contrary to merely material logic, the *inside* of this magnificent gallery, which is both spiritual and religious, is much, much larger and grander than what is outside. I hope and pray that my readers will one day discover that for themselves.

Appendix

For those readers who wish to explore more concretely the Christian answers to religious questions, we recommend the following resources:

Theology and Sanity by Frank Sheed

Mere Christianity by C. S. Lewis

Chance or the Dance? by Thomas Howard

Catholic and Christian by Peter Kreeft

YouCat by Christoph Cardinal Schönborn

About the Author

Fr. John Bartunek, LC, S.Th.D, received his BA in History from Stanford University in 1990. He comes from an evangelical Christian background and became a member of the Catholic Church in 1991. After spending time as a teacher, coach, and actor, he entered the religious Congregation of the Legionaries of Christ in 1993 and was ordained in 2003, and earned his doctorate in moral theology in 2010. He provided spiritual support on the set of Mel Gibson's "The Passion of the Christ." His most widely known book is called *The Better Part: A Christ-Centered Resource for Personal Prayer*. Fr. John has contributed news commentary regarding religious issues on NBC, CNN, Fox, and the BBC. He currently resides in Michigan, where he continues his writing apostolate and serves as a confessor and spiritual director.